STYLE GUIDE

OTHER ECONOMIST BOOKS

Guide to Analysing Companies
Guide to Business Modelling
Guide to Business Planning
Guide to Economic Indicators
Guide to the European Union
Guide to Financial Markets
Guide to Management Ideas
Numbers Guide

Dictionary of Business
Dictionary of Economics
International Dictionary of Finance

Brands and Branding
Business Consulting
Business Ethics
Business Miscellany
Business Strategy
China's Stockmarket
Dealing with Financial Risk
Future of Technology
Globalisation
Headhunters and How to Use Them
Successful Mergers
The City
Wall Street

Essential Director
Essential Economics
Essential Finance
Essential Internet
Essential Investment
Essential Negotiation

Pocket World in Figures

The
Economist

STYLE GUIDE

THE ECONOMIST IN ASSOCIATION WITH
PROFILE BOOKS LTD

Published by Profile Books Ltd,
3A Exmouth Street, Pine Street, London EC1R 0JH
www.profilebooks.com

The greatest care has been taken in compiling this book.
However, no responsibility can be accepted by the publishers or compilers
for the accuracy of the information presented.

Typeset in EcoType by MacGuru Ltd
info@macguru.org.uk

Printed in Great Britain by
Clays, Bungay, Suffolk

A CIP catalogue record for this book is available
from the British Library

ISBN 978 1 86197 916 2

The paper this book is printed on is certified by the © 1996 Forest
Stewardship Council A.C. (FSC). It is ancient-forest friendly. The printer holds
FSC chain of custody SGS-COC-2061

FSC
Mixed Sources
Product group from well-managed
forests and other controlled sources
Cert no. SGS-COC-2061
www.fsc.org
© 1996 Forest Stewardship Council

Contents

Preface

Every newspaper has its own style book, a set of rules telling journalists whether to write e-mail or email, Gadaffi or Qaddafi, judgement or judgment. *The Economist's* style book does this and a bit more. It also warns writers of some common mistakes and encourages them to write with clarity and simplicity.

All the prescriptive judgments in the style guide are directly derived from those used each week in writing and editing *The Economist.*

This ninth edition of the "The Economist Style Guide" is in three parts. The first is based on the style book used by those who edit *The Economist*; it is largely the work of John Grimond, who has over the years been Britain, American and foreign editor. The second, on American and British English, describes some of the main differences between the two great English-speaking areas, in spelling, grammar and usage.

To make the style guide of greater general interest, Part 3 consists of information drawing on the reference books published under The Economist Books imprint and expanded to include handy reference material that might appeal to readers of *The Economist.* Such information is checked and new matter included for every new edition. For this edition the text in Part 3 has been extensively reviewed and reorganised to make the book more modern and up to date.

Throughout the text, italic type is used for examples except where they are presented in lists, when the type is Roman, as this text is. Words in bold indicate a separate but relevant entry, that is, a cross-reference. Small capitals are used only in the way *The Economist* uses them, for which see the entries **abbreviations** and **capitals**.

Introduction

On only two scores can *The Economist* hope to outdo its rivals consistently. One is the quality of its analysis; the other is the quality of its writing. The aim of this book is to give some general advice on writing, to point out some common errors and to set some arbitrary rules.

The first requirement of *The Economist* is that it should be readily understandable. Clarity of writing usually follows clarity of thought. So think what you want to say, then say it as simply as possible. Keep in mind George Orwell's six elementary rules ("Politics and the English Language", 1946):

1. Never use a metaphor, simile or other figure of speech which you are used to seeing in print (*see* **metaphors**).
2. Never use a long word where a short one will do (*see* **short words**).
3. If it is possible to cut out a word, always cut it out (*see* **unnecessary words**).
4. Never use the passive where you can use the active (*see* **grammar and syntax**).
5. Never use a foreign phrase, a scientific word or a jargon word if you can think of an everyday English equivalent (*see* **jargon**).
6. Break any of these rules sooner than say anything outright barbarous (*see* **iconoclasm**).

Readers are primarily interested in what you have to say. By the way in which you say it you may encourage them either to read on or to give up. If you want them to read on:

Do not be stuffy "To write a genuine, familiar or truly English style", said Hazlitt, "is to write as anyone would speak in common conversation who had a thorough command or choice of words or who could discourse with ease, force and perspicuity setting aside all pedantic and oratorical flourishes."

Use the language of everyday speech, not that of spokesmen, lawyers or bureaucrats (so prefer *let* to *permit*, *people* to *persons*, *buy* to *purchase*, *colleague* to *peer*, *way out* to *exit*, *present* to *gift*, *rich* to *wealthy*, *show* to *demonstrate*, *break* to *violate*). Pomposity and long-windedness tend to obscure meaning, or reveal the lack of it: strip them away in favour of plain words.

Do not be hectoring or arrogant Those who disagree with you are not necessarily *stupid* or *insane*. Nobody needs to be described as silly: let your analysis show that he is. When you express opinions, do not simply make assertions. The aim is not just to tell readers what you think, but to persuade them; if you use arguments, reasoning and evidence, you may succeed. Go easy on the oughts and shoulds.

Do not be too pleased with yourself Don't boast of your own cleverness by telling readers that you correctly predicted something or that you have a scoop. You are more likely to bore or irritate them than to impress them.

Do not be too chatty *Surprise, surprise* is more irritating than informative. So is *Ho, ho* and, in the middle of a sentence, *wait for it*, etc.

Do not be too didactic If too many sentences begin *Compare, Consider, Expect, Imagine, Look at, Note, Prepare for, Remember* or *Take*, readers will think they are reading a textbook (or, indeed, a style book).

Do your best to be lucid ("I see but one rule: to be clear", Stendhal) Simple sentences help. Keep complicated constructions and gimmicks to a minimum, if necessary by remembering the *New Yorker*'s comment: "Backward ran sentences until reeled the mind." The following letter from a reader may be chastening:

Sir
At times just one sentence in *The Economist* can give us hours of enjoyment, such as "Yet German diplomats in Belgrade failed to persuade their government that it was wrong to think that the threat of international recognition of Croatia and Slovenia would itself deter Serbia."

During my many years as a reader of your newspaper, I have distilled two lessons about the use of our language. Firstly, it is usually easier to write a double negative than it is to interpret it. Secondly, unless the description of an event which is considered to be not without consequence includes a double or higher-order negative, then it cannot be disproven that the writer has neglected to eliminate other interpretations of the event which are not satisfactory in light of other possibly not unrelated events which might not have occurred at all.

For these reasons, I have not neglected your timely reminder that I ought not to let my subscription lapse. It certainly cannot be said that I am an unhappy reader.
Willard Dunning

Mark Twain described how a good writer treats sentences: "At times he may indulge himself with a long one, but he will make sure there are no folds in it, no vaguenesses, no parenthetical interruptions of its view as a whole; when he has done with it, it won't be a sea-serpent with half of its arches under the water; it will be a torch-light procession."

Long paragraphs, like long sentences, can confuse the reader. "The paragraph", according to Fowler, "is essentially a unit of thought, not of length; it must be homogeneous in subject matter and sequential in treatment." One-sentence paragraphs should be used only occasionally.

Clear thinking is the key to clear writing. "A scrupulous writer", observed Orwell, "in every sentence that he writes will ask himself at least four questions, thus: What am I trying to say? What words will express it? What image or idiom will make it clearer? Is this image fresh enough to have an effect? And he will probably ask himself two more: Could I put it more shortly? Have I said anything that is avoidably ugly?"

Scrupulous writers will also notice that their copy is edited only lightly and is likely to be used. It may even be read.

A note on editing

Editing has always made a large contribution to *The Economist*'s excellence. It should continue to do so. But editing on a screen is beguilingly simple. It is quite easy to rewrite an article without realising that one has done much to it at all: the cursor leaves no trace of crossings-out, handwritten insertions, rearranged sentences or reordered paragraphs. The temptation is to continue to make changes until something emerges that the editor himself might have written. One benefit of this is a tightly edited newspaper. One cost is a certain sameness. The risk is that the newspaper will turn into a collection of 70 or 80 articles which read as though they have been written by no more than half a dozen hands.

The Economist has a single editorial outlook, and it is anonymous. But it is the work of many people, both in London and abroad, as its datelines testify. If the prose of our Tokyo correspondent is indistinguishable from the prose of our Nairobi correspondent, readers will feel they are being robbed of variety. They may also wonder whether these two people really exist, or whether the entire newspaper is not written in London.

The moral for editors is that they should respect good writing. That is mainly what this style sheet is designed to promote. It is not intended to impose a single style on all *The Economist*'s journalists. A writer's style, after all, should reflect his mind and personality. So long as they are compatible with *The Economist*'s editorial outlook, and so long as the prose is good, editors should exercise suitable self-restraint. Remember that your copy, too, will be edited. And even if you think you are not guilty, bear in mind this comment from John Gross:

> Most writers I know have tales to tell of being mangled by editors and mauled by fact-checkers, and naturally it is the flagrant instances they choose to single out - absurdities, outright distortions of meaning, glaring errors. But most of the damage done is a good deal less spectacular. It consists of small changes (usually too boring to describe to anyone else) that flatten a writer's style, slow down his argument, neutralise his irony; that ruin the rhythm of a sentence or the balance of paragraph; that deaden the tone that makes the music. I sometimes think of the process as one of "desophistication".

John Grimond

part 1

the essence of style

a or the *see* **grammar and syntax**.

abbreviations

Unless an abbreviation (or acronym) is so familiar that it is used more often than the full form:

AIDS BBC CIA EU FBI HIV IMF NATO NGO OECD UNESCO

or unless the full form would provide little illumination – *AWACS, DNA* – write the words in full on first appearance: thus, Trades Union Congress (not *TUC*). If in doubt about its familiarity, explain what the organisation is or does. After the first mention, try not to repeat the abbreviation too often; so write *the agency* rather than *the IAEA, the party* rather than *the KMT*, to avoid spattering the page with capital letters. There is no need to give the initials of an organisation if it is not referred to again.

Do not use spatterings of abbreviations and acronyms simply in order to cram more words in; you will end up irritating readers rather than informing them. An article in a recent issue of *The Economist* contained the following:

CIA DCI DNI DOD DVD FBI NCTC NSA

The article immediately following had:

CTAC CX DIS FCO GCHQ IT JIC JTAC MI5 MI6 MP SCOPE WMD

Some of these are well known to most readers and can readily be held in the mind. But unfamiliar abbreviations may oblige the reader to be constantly referring back to the first use. Better to repeat some names in full, or to write *the agency, the committee, the party*, etc, than to allow an undisciplined proliferation. And prefer *chief executive* or *boss* to *CEO*.

ampersands should be used:
1   when they are part of the name of a company:
    Procter & Gamble Pratt & Whitney
2   for such things as constituencies where two names are linked to form one unit:
    The rest of Brighouse & Spenborough joins with the Batley part of Batley & Morley to form Batley & Spen.
    The area thus became the Pakistani province of Kashmir and the Indian state of Jammu & Kashmir.
3   in R&D and S&L.

definite article If an abbreviation can be pronounced – EFTA, NATO, UNESCO – it does not generally require the definite article. Other organisations, except companies, should usually be preceded by *the*:

the BBC *the* KGB *the* NHS *the* NIESR *the* UNHCR

elements do not take small caps when abbreviated:

carbon dioxide is CO_2
chlorofluorocarbons are CFCs
lead is Pb
methane is CH_4
the oxides of nitrogen are generally NOX

Different isotopes of the same element are distinguished by raised (superscript) prefixes:

carbon-14 is ^{14}C
helium-3 is ^{3}He

headings, cross-heads, captions, etc In headings, rubrics, cross-heads, footnotes, captions, tables, charts (including sources), use ordinary caps, not small caps.

initials in people's and companies' names take points (with a space between initials and name, but not between initials). In general, follow the practice preferred by people, companies and organisations in writing their own names.

F.W. de Klerk E.I. Du Pont de Nemours V.P. Singh F.W. Woolworth

junior and senior Spell out in full (and lower case) *junior* and *senior* after a name:

George Bush junior George Bush senior

lower case Abbreviate:

kilograms (not *kilogrammes*) to *kg* (or *kilos*)
kilometres per hour to *kph*
kilometres to *km*
miles per hour to *mph*

Use lower case for *kg, km, lb* (never *lbs*), *mph* and other measures, and for *ie, eg*, which should both be followed by commas. When used with figures, these lower-case abbreviations should follow immediately, with no space:

11am 4.30pm 15kg 35mm 100mph 78rpm

Two abbreviations together, however, must be separated: *60m b/d*. Use *b/d* not *bpd* as an abbreviation for *barrels per day*.

MPs Except in British contexts, use *MP* only after first spelling out member of Parliament in full (in many places an *MP* is a military policeman).

Members of the *Scottish Parliament* are *MSPs*.
Members of the *European Parliament* are *MEPs* (not Euro-*MPs*).

organisations

EFTA is the *European Free Trade Association*.
IDA is the *International Development Association*.
NAFTA is the *North American Free-Trade Agreement*.
The *FAO* is the *Food and Agriculture Organisation*.
The *FDA* is the *Food and Drug Administration*.
The *PLO* is the *Palestine Liberation Organisation*.

pronounceable abbreviations

Abbreviations that can be pronounced and are composed of bits of words rather than just initials should be spelt out in upper and lower case:

Cocom	Mercosur	Unicef
Frelimo	Nepad	Unisom
Kfor	Renamo	Unprofor
Legco	Sfor	

Trips (trade-related aspects of intellectual property rights)

There is generally no need for more than one initial capital letter, unless the word is a company or a trade name: *MiG, ConsGold*.

ranks and titles Do not use *Prof, Sen, Col*, etc. *Lieut-Colonel* and *Lieut-Commander* are permissible. So is *Rev*, but it must be preceded by the and followed by a Christian name or initial: *the Rev Jesse Jackson* (thereafter *Mr Jackson*).

scientific units named after individuals Most scientific units, except those of temperature, that are named after individuals, should be set in small capitals, though any attachments denoting multiples go in lower case:

ampère is A or *amp*
öhm is O
watt is W
kilowatt, 1,000 watts, is kW
milliwatt, one-thousandth of a watt, is mW
megawatt, 1m watts, is MW

small caps usage

1. In the text abbreviations, whether they can be pronounced as words or not:

    GNP GDP FOB CIF A-levels D-marks T-shirts X-rays

    should be set in small capitals, with no points, unless they are currencies like *Nkr* or *SFr*, elements like H and O or degrees of temperature like °F and °C.

2. Brackets, apostrophes and all other typographical furniture accompanying small capitals are generally set in ordinary roman, with a lower-case s (also roman) for plurals and genitives: IOUs, MPs' salaries, SDRs, etc.

3. Ampersands are set as small capitals, as are numerals and any hyphens attaching them to a small capital (*see also* below). Thus:

    R&D A23 M1 F-16

4. AD and BC (76AD, 55BC): figures and numbers thus joined should both be set in small capitals.

5. Abbreviations that include upper-case and lower-case

letters must be set in a mixture of small capitals and roman: *BPhils, PhDs*.

6   Do not use small caps for **roman numerals**.

writing out upper-case abbreviations Most upper-case abbreviations take upper-case initial letters when written in full. The *LSO* is the London Symphony Orchestra. However, there are exceptions:

CAP but *common agricultural policy*
EMU but *economic and monetary union*
GDP but *gross domestic product*
PSBR but *public-sector borrowing requirement*
VLSI but *very large-scale integration*

miscellaneous Spell out:

page pages hectares miles

Remember, too, that the V of *HIV* stands for virus, so do not write *HIV virus*.

See **measures** in Part 3.

absent In Latin *absent* is a verb meaning *they are away*. In English it is either an adjective (*absent friends*) or a verb (*to absent yourself*). It is not a preposition meaning *in the absence of*.

accents On words now accepted as English, use accents only when they make a crucial difference to pronunciation:

café cliché communiqué exposé façade soupçon

But: *chateau decor elite feted naive*

The main accents and diacritical signs are:

acute	république
grave	grand'mère
circumflex	bête noire
umlaut	Länder, Österreich (Austria)
cedilla	français
tilde	señor, São Paulo

If you use one accent (except the tilde – strictly, a diacritical sign), use all:

émigré mêlée protégé résumé

Put the accents and diacritical signs on French, German, Spanish and Portuguese names and words:

José Manuel Barroso   Françoise de Panafieu
Federico Peña   Wolfgang Schäuble

Leave accents and diacritical signs off other foreign names. Any foreign word in italics should, however, be given its proper accents. (*See also* **italics**.)

acronym A pronounceable word, formed from the initials of other words, like *radar* or *NATO*. It is not a set of initials, like the *BBC* or the *IMF*.

actionable means *giving ground for a lawsuit*. Do not use it to mean *susceptible of being put into practice*: prefer *practical*.

active, not passive Be direct. *A hit B* describes the event more concisely than *B was hit by A*.

adjectives and adverbs *see* **grammar and syntax, punctuation**.

adjectives of proper nouns *see* **grammar and syntax, punctuation**.

address What did journalists and politicians do in the days, not so long ago, when *address* was used as a verb only before objects such as *audience, letter, ball, haggis* and, occasionally, *themselves*? Questions can be *answered*, issues *discussed*, problems *solved*, difficulties *dealt with*. See **clichés**.

aetiology is the *science of causation*, or *an inquiry into something's origins*. Etiolate is to *make* or *become pale for lack of light*.

affect the verb, means to have an influence on, as in *the novel affected his attitude to immigrants*. See also **effect**.

affirmative action is a euphemism, uglier even than *human-rights abuses* and more obscure even than *comfort station*, with little to be said for it. It is too late to suppress it altogether and perhaps too soon to consign it to the midden of civil-rights studies, but try to avoid it as much as possible. If you cannot escape it, put it in quotation marks on first mention and, unless the context makes its meaning clear, explain what it is. You may, however, find that *preferential treatment, job preferment* or even *discrimination* serve just as well as alternatives. *See* **euphemisms**.

affordable By whom? Avoid *affordable housing, affordable computers* and other unthinking uses of advertising lingo.

Afghan names *see* **names**.

aggravate means *make worse*, not *irritate* or *annoy*.

aggression is an unattractive quality, so do not call a *keen* salesman an aggressive one (unless his foot is in the door).

agony column Remember that when Sherlock Holmes perused this, it was a *personal column*. Only recently has it come to mean *letters to an agony aunt*.

agree Things are agreed *on, to* or *about*, not just agreed.

alibi An *alibi* is the fact of being elsewhere, not a false explanation.

alternate, alternative *Alternate* (as an adjective) means *every other*. *Alternative* (as a noun), strictly, means one of two, not one of three, four, five or more (which may be *options*). As an adjective, *alternative* means *of two* (or, loosely, *more*) *things*, or *possible as an alternative*.

Americanisms Many American words and expressions have passed into the language; others have vigour, particularly if used sparingly. Some are short and to the point, so for example prefer *lay off* to *make redundant*.

   Spat and *scam*, two words beloved by some journalists, have the merit of brevity, but so do *row* and *fraud*; *squabble* and *swindle* might sometimes be used instead. But many words favoured in American English usage are unnecessarily long, or unusual, so use:

and not *additionally*
the army not the *military* (noun)
car not *automobile*

company not *corporation*
court not *courtroom* or *courthouse*
district not *neighbourhood*
normality not *normalcy*
oblige not *obligate*
rocket not *skyrocket*
speciality not *specialty*
stocks not *inventories*, unless there is the risk of confusion with
    stocks and shares
transport not *transportation*

Other Americanisms are euphemistic or obscure, so avoid:

affirmative action	point men
ball games	rookies
end runs	stand-off

adverbs Put adverbs where you would put them in normal
    speech, which is usually after the verb (not before it, which
    usually is where Americans put them).

avoiding nouning adjectives Similarly, do not noun adjectives
    such as:

advisory – prefer *warning*
centennial – prefer *centenary*
inaugural – prefer *inauguration*
meet (noun) – *meeting* is better
spend (noun) – *spending* is preferable

avoiding verbing and adjectiving nouns Try not to verb nouns
    or to adjective them. So do not:

access files
author books (still less *co-author* them)
critique style guides
gun someone down, use *shoot*
haemorrhage red ink (haemorrhage is a noun)
let one event *impact* another
loan money
pressure colleagues (*press* will do)
progress reports
source inputs
trial programmes

Avoid *parenting* (or using the word) and *parenting skills*.
(*See also* **grammar and syntax**.)

And though it is sometimes necessary to use nouns as adjectives, there is no need to call:

an *attempted coup* a *coup attempt*
a *suspected terrorist* a *terrorist suspect*
the *Californian legislature* the *California legislature*

Vilest of all is the habit of throwing together several nouns into one ghastly adjectival reticule:

Texas millionaire real-estate developer and failed thrift entrepreneur Hiram Turnipseed ...

coining words Avoid coining verbs and adjectives unnecessarily. Instead of:

dining experiences and *writing experiences*: use *dining* and *writing*
downplaying criticism, you can *play* it *down* (or perhaps *minimise* it)
skiing Vail, *ski at* Vail
upcoming and *ongoing* are better put as *forthcoming* and *continuing*
Why *outfit* your children when you can *fit* them *out*?

old-fashioned terms Some American expressions that were once common in English English (and some still used in Scottish English) now sound old-fashioned to most British ears. So prefer:

clothes or *clothing* to *apparel* or *garments*
doctors to *physicians*
got to *gotten*
lawyers to *attorneys*
often to *oftentimes*
over or *too* to *overly*

overuse of American words Do not feel obliged to follow American fashion in overusing such words as:

constituency – try *supporters*
gubernatorial – this means "relating to a governor"
perception – try *belief* or *view*

rhetoric (of which there is too little, not too much) – try *language* or *speeches* or *exaggeration* if that is what you mean

some differences In an American context you may *run* for office (but please *stand* in countries with parliamentary systems) and your car may sometimes run on *gasoline* instead of *petrol*. But if you use *corn* in the American sense you should explain that this is *maize* to most people (unless it is an *old chestnut*).

Slate can also mean *abuse* (as a verb) but does not, in Britain, mean *predict, schedule* or *nominate*. And if you must use American expressions, use them correctly (a *rain-check* does not imply checking on the weather outside).

In Britain:

Cars are *hired*, not *rented*, and are left in *car parks*, not *parking lots*.

City centres are not *central cities*.

Companies: *call for* a record profit if you wish to exhort the workers, but not if you merely predict one. And do not *post* it if it has been achieved. If it has not, look for someone new to *head*, not *head up*, the company.

Countries, nations and states: London is the *country*'s capital, not the *nation*'s. If you wish to build a *nation*, you will *bind its peoples together*; if you wish to build a *state*, you will forge its *institutions*.

Deep: make a *deep* study or even a study *in depth*, but not an *in-depth* study.

Ex-servicemen are not necessarily *veterans*.

Football for most people is a *game* – you do not have to call it a *sport* – that Americans call *soccer*.

Do not *figure out* if you can *work out*.

Fresh should be used of vegetables, not teenagers.

Grow a beard or a tomato but not a company (or indeed a salesman: the *Financial Times* reported on August 8th 2003 that BMW was "to grow its own car salesmen").

Hikes are *walks*, not *increases*.

Hospital: when we are seriously ill we are *in hospital*, not *in the hospital*, still less *hospitalised*.

Do not use *likely* to mean *probably*.

Make a *rumpus* rather than a *ruckus*, be *rumbustious* rather than *rambunctious*, and *snigger* rather than *snicker*.

On-site inspections are allowed, but not *on-train teams* or *in-ear headphones*.

Outside America, nowadays, you stay *outside* the door, not
outside of it.

Programme: you may *program* a computer but in all other
contexts the word is *programme*.

Keep a promise, rather than *deliver on* it.

Raise cattle and pigs, but children are (or should be) *brought up*.

Regular is not a synonym for *ordinary* or *normal*: Mussolini
brought in the *regular* train, All-Bran the *regular* man; it is
quite *normal* to be without either.

A *religious group* sounds better than a *faith-based organisation*.

Scenarios are best kept for the theatre, *postures* for the gym,
parameters for the parabola.

School: children are *at* school, not *in* it.

Do not *task* people, or *meet with* them.

Throw *stones*, not *rock*.

Trains run from *railway stations*, not *train stations*. The people
in them, and on buses, are *passengers*, not *riders*.

Use *senior* rather than *ranking*.

And only the speechless are *dumb*, the well-dressed (and a
few devices) *smart* and the insane *mad*.

tenses Choose tenses according to British usage, too. In particular,
do not fight shy – as Americans often do – of the perfect tense,
especially where no date or time is given. Thus:

Mr Bush has woken up to the danger is preferable to *Mr Bush
woke up to the danger*, unless you can add *last week* or *when he
heard the explosion*.

Do not write *Your salary just got smaller* or *I shrunk the
kids*. In British English *Your salary has just got smaller* and *I've
shrunk the kids*.

See *also* **adjectives of proper nouns**, **euphemisms**, **grammar and
syntax**, and Part 2.

aircraft *see* **hyphens** and **italics**.

among and between Some sticklers insist that, where division
is involved, *among* should be used where three or more are
concerned, *between* where only two are concerned. So:

The plum jobs were shared among the Socialists, the Liberals and

*the Christian Democrats, while the president and the vice-president
divided the cash between themselves.*

This distinction is unnecessary. But take care with *between*. To
fall between two stools, however painful, is grammatically acceptable;
to fall between the cracks is to challenge the laws of physics.

Prefer *among* to *amongst*.

an should be used before a word beginning with a vowel sound (*an
egg, an umbrella, an MP*) or an h if, and only if, the h is silent (*an
honorary degree*). But *a European, a university, a U-turn, a hospital,
a hotel. Historical* is an exception: it is preceded by *an*, the h
remaining silent.

anarchy means the *complete absence of law or government*. It may be
harmonious or chaotic.

animals For the spelling of the Latin names of animals, plants, etc, *see*
Latin names.

annus horribilis, annus mirabilis *Annus* horribilis is often used,
presumably in contrast to *annus mirabilis*, to describe an *awful
year*, for example by Queen Elizabeth in 1992 (the year of her
daughter's divorce, the separation of the Duke and Duchess of
York and a fire at Windsor Castle) and by Kofi Annan in 2004 (a
year of scandal and controversy at the United Nations). It serves
its purpose well, but it should be noted that *annus mirabilis*
originally meant much the same thing: 1666, of which it was first
used, was the year of the great fire of London and the second
year of the great plague in England, although English spirits were
lifted a bit by a defeat of the Dutch navy. Physicists, however,
have latterly used the term to describe 1932, the year in which
the neutron was discovered, the positron identified and the
atomic nucleus first broken up artificially. And Philip Larkin, more
understandably, used it to describe 1963, the year in which sexual
intercourse began.

anon means *soon*, though it once meant *straight away*. *Presently* also
means *soon*, though it is increasingly misused to mean *now*. (*See
also* **presently**.)

anticipate does not mean *expect*. Jack and Jill expected to marry; if they anticipated marriage, only Jill might find herself expectant.

apostasy, heresy If you abandon your religion, you commit *apostasy*. If that religion is the prevailing one in your community and your beliefs are contrary to its orthodoxy, you commit *heresy*.

apostrophes *see* **punctuation**.

appeal is intransitive nowadays (except in America), so appeal *against decisions*.

appraise means *set a price on*. *Apprise* means *inform*.

Arabic The Arabic alphabet has several consonants which have no exact equivalents in English: for example, a hard *t* as well as a normal soft one, a hard *s* as well as a soft one, two different (one vocalised, the other not) *th* sounds. Moreover, there are three sounds – a glottal stop like a hiccup, a glottal sound akin to strangulation and a uvular trill like a Frenchman gargling. Ultra-fastidious transliterators try to reproduce these subtleties with a profusion of apostrophes and *h*s which yield spellings like Mu'ammar al-Qadhdhafi. The risk of error and the sheer ugliness on the page are too great to justify the effort, so usually ignore the differences.

Vowels present a lesser problem. There are only three – *a, u, i* – but each can be lengthened. Do not bother to differentiate between the short and the long *a*. Occasionally, a spelling is established where the *u* has been lengthened by using *oo*, as in *Sultan Qaboos*. In such instances, follow that convention, but in general go for *ou*, as in *murabitoun* or *Ibn Khaldoun*. For a long *i* you should normally use *ee* (as in *mujahideen*).

Muhammad is the correct spelling unless it is part of the name of someone who spells it differently. (*See also* **names**.)

as of say, April 5th or April. Prefer *on* (or *after*, or *since*) April 5th, in April.

assassinate is, properly, the term used not just for any old killing, but for the murder of a prominent person, usually for a political purpose.

as to There is usually a more appropriate preposition than *as to*.

autarchy, autarky *Autarchy* means absolute sovereignty. *Autarky* means self-sufficiency.

avocation An *avocation* is a distraction or *diversion from your ordinary employment*, not a synonym for *vocation*.

bail, bale In the hayfield, *bale*; otherwise *bail*, *bail out* and *bail-out* (noun).

Bangladeshi names *see* **names.**

-based A *Paris-based group* may be all right, if, say, that group operates abroad (otherwise just say a *group in Paris*). But avoid *community-based, faith-based, knowledge-based*, etc. A *community-based organisation* is perhaps a *community organisation*; a *faith-based organisation* is probably a *church* (or might it be the Labour or Republican Party?); a *knowledge-based industry* needs explanation: all industries depend on knowledge.

beg the question means neither *raise the question, invite the question* nor *evade the answer*. To *beg the question* is to adopt an argument whose conclusion depends upon assuming the truth of the very conclusion the argument is designed to produce.

All governments should promote free trade because otherwise protectionism will increase. This begs the question.

Belarusian names *see* **names.**

bellwether This is the leading sheep of a flock, on whose neck a bell is hung. It is nothing to do with climate, prevailing winds or the like, but the term is used in the stockmarket.

between *see* **among and between.**

biannual, biennial *Biannual* can mean twice a year or once every two years. Avoid. Since *biennial* also means once every two years, that is best avoided too.

bicentennial Prefer bicentenary (as a noun).

black *In the black* means *in profit* in Britain, but *making losses* in some places. Use *in profit*.

blooded, bloodied *Blooded* means *pedigreed* (as in *blue*-blooded) or *initiated*. *Bloodied* means *wounded*.

bon vivant not *bon viveur*.

both ... and A preposition placed after *both* should be repeated after *and*. Thus *both to right and to left;* but *to both right and left* is all right.

brackets *see* **punctuation**.

British titles *see* **titles**.

brokerage is what a stockbroking firm does, not what it is.

by contrast, in contrast Use *by contrast* only when you are comparing one thing with another: *Somalia is a poor country. By contrast, Egypt is rich.* This means Egypt is rich by comparision with Somalia, though by other standards it is poor. If you are simply noting a difference, say *in contrast: Tony Blair takes his holidays in Tuscany. In contrast, Gordon Brown goes to Kirkaldy.*

C

cadre Keep this word for the *framework of a military unit* or the *officers of such a unit*, not for a *communist functionary*.

calibres *see* **hyphens.**

Cambodian names *see* **names.**

Canute's exercise on the seashore was designed to persuade his courtiers of what he knew to be true but they doubted, ie, that he was not omnipotent. Don't imply he was surprised to get his feet wet.

capitals A balance has to be struck between so many capitals that the eyes dance and so few that the reader is diverted more by our style than by our substance. The general rules are to dignify with capital letters organisations and institutions, but not people; and full names, but not informal ones. More exact rules are laid out below. Even these, however, leave some decisions to individual judgment. If in doubt use lower case unless it looks absurd. And remember that "a foolish consistency is the hobgoblin of little minds" (Emerson).

avoiding confusion Use capitals to avoid confusion, especially with no (and therefore yes). *In Bergen no votes predominated* suggests a stalemate, whereas *In Bergen No votes predominated* suggests a triumph of noes over yeses. In most contexts, though, yes and no should be lower case: "The answer is no."

Organisations with unusual or misleading names, such as the *African National Congress* and *Civic Forum*, may become the *Congress* and the *Forum* on second and subsequent mentions.

cities *City* with a capital, even though *City* is not an integral part of their names:

Guatemala City	New York City
Ho Chi Minh City	Panama City
Kuwait City	Quebec City
Mexico City	

City also takes a capital when it is part of the name:

Dodge City	Quezon City
Kansas City	Salt Lake City
Oklahoma City	

compass points Lower case for:

east   west   north   south

except when part of a name (*North Korea, South Africa, West End*) or part of a thinking group: *the South, the Mid-West, the West* (but lower case for vaguer areas such as the American *north-east, north-west, south-east, south-west*).

If you are, say, comparing regions some of which would normally be upper case and some lower case, and it would look odd to leave them that way, put them all lower case:

House prices in the north-east and the south are rising faster than those in the mid-west and the south-west.

The regions of Africa are *southern, east, west* and *north Africa.* But *South Africa* is the name of the country.

The *third world* (an unsatisfactory term now that the communist second world has disappeared) is lower case.

Europe Europe's divisions are no longer neatly political, and are now geographically imprecise, so use lower case for *central, eastern* and *western Europe.*

Use *West Germany* (*West Berlin*) and *East Germany* (*East Berlin*) only in historical references. They are now *west* or *western Germany* (*Berlin*) and *east* or *eastern Germany* (*eastern Berlin*).

The *Basque country* (or *region*) is ill-defined and contentious, and may include parts of both France and Spain, so lower case for country (or region).

Euro-terms The usual rules apply for the full, proper names (with informal equivalents on the right below). Thus:

European Commission	the commission
European Parliament	the parliament
European Union	the Union
Treaty of Rome	the Rome treaty
Treaty on European Union	the Maastricht treaty

The EU grouping may be called EU-15, EU-25

When making *Euro-* or *euro-words*, always introduce a hyphen, except for *Europhile*, *Europhobe* and *Eurosceptic*. Prefer *euro zone* or *euro area* (two words, no hyphen) to *euro-land*.

Eurobond
Euroyen bond
CAP is the *common agricultural policy.*
EMU stands for *economic and* (not European) *monetary union.*
ERM is the *exchange-rate mechanism.*
IGC is an *inter-governmental conference.*

finance In finance there are particular exceptions to the general rule of initial caps for full names, lower case for informal ones. There are also rules about what to do on second mention.

Deutschmarks are still known just as *D-marks*, even though all references are historical.

Special drawing rights are lower case but are abbreviated as SDR.

The *Bank of England* and its foreign equivalents have initial caps when named formally and separately, but collectively they are central banks in lower case, except those like Brazil's and Ireland's, which are actually named the *Central Bank.* The *Bank of England* becomes the *bank* on second mention.

The *IMF* may become the *fund* on second mention.

The *World Bank* and the *Fed* (after first spelling it out as the *Federal Reserve*) take initial upper case, although these are shortened, informal names. The *World Bank* becomes the *bank* on second mention.

Treasury bonds issued by America's Treasury should be upper case; *treasury bills* (or *bonds*) of a general kind should be lower case. Avoid T-*bonds* and t-*bills*.

historical terms

Black Death	Reconstruction
Cultural Revolution	Renaissance
the Depression	Restoration
Holocaust (Hitler's)	Thirty Years War
Middle Ages	Year of the Dog (but new year)
New Deal	

labels formed from proper names A political, economic or religious label formed from a proper name should have a capital:

Buddhism	Leninist
Christian	Luddite
Finlandisation	Maronite
Gaullism	Marxist
Hindu	Napoleonic
Hobbesian	Paisleyite
Islamic	Thatcherism
Jacobite	

Note that Indian castes are lower-case italic, except for brahmin, which has now become an English word and is therefore lower-case roman (unless it is mentioned along with several other less familiar caste names in italic).

organisations, institutions, acts, etc

1 Organisations, ministries, departments, treaties, acts, etc, generally take upper case when their full name (or something pretty close to it, eg, *State Department*) is used.

Amnesty International
Arab League
Bank of England (the bank)
Central Committee
Court of Appeal
the Crown (Britain)
Department for Environment, Food & Rural Affairs (DEFRA)
Department of State (the department)
European Commission
Forestry Commission
Health and Safety at Work Act

High Court
House of Commons
House of Lords
House of Representatives
Household Cavalry
Metropolitan Police
Ministry of Defence
New York Stock Exchange
Oxford University
Politburo
Scottish Parliament (the parliament)
Senate
St Paul's Cathedral (the cathedral)
Supreme Court
Treasury
Treaty of Rome
Welsh Assembly (the assembly)
World Bank (the bank)

2 Organisations with unusual or misleading names, such as
the *African National Congress* and *Civic Forum*, may become
the *Congress* and the *Forum* on second and subsequent
mentions.

3 But most other organisations – agencies, banks, commissions
(including the *European Commission* and the *European Union*),
etc – take lower case when referred to incompletely on second
mention.

4 Informal names
Organisations, committees, commissions, special groups, etc,
that are impermanent, ad hoc, local or relatively insignificant
should be lower case:

international economic subcommittee of the Senate Foreign
      Relations Committee
Market Blandings rural district council
Oxford University bowls club
subcommittee on journalists' rights of the National Executive
      Committee of the Labour Party

5 Rough descriptions or translations
Use lower case for rough descriptions (*the safety act*, the
American health department, the *French parliament*, as distinct

from its National Assembly). If you are not sure whether the English translation of a foreign name is exact or not, assume it is rough and use lower case.

6 Congress and Parliament
Congress and Parliament are upper case, unless parliament is used not to describe the institution but the period of time for which it sits.

This bill will not be brought forward until the next parliament.

But congressional and parliamentary are lower case, as is the opposition, even when used in the sense of her majesty's loyal opposition.
The government, the administration and the cabinet are always lower case.
After first mention, the House of Commons (or Lords, or Representatives) becomes the House.

7 Acts
In America acts given the names of their sponsors (eg, Glass-Steagall, Helms-Burton) are always rough descriptions (see above) and so take a lower-case act.

people
1 Ranks and titles
Use upper case when written in conjunction with a name, but lower case when on their own:

Colonel Qaddafi, but the colonel
Pope John Paul, but the pope
President Bush, but the president
Queen Elizabeth, but the queen
Vice-President Cheney, but the vice-president

Do not write Prime Minister Blair or Defence Secretary Rumsfeld; they are the prime minister, Mr Blair, and the defence secretary, Mr Rumsfeld. You might, however, write Chancellor Schröder.

2 Office-holders
When referred to merely by their office, not by their name, office-holders are lower case:

the chairman of British Airways
the chancellor of the exchequer

the foreign secretary
the president of the United States
the prime minister
the speaker
the treasury secretary

The only exceptions are a few titles that would look unduly peculiar without capitals:

Black Rod
Chancellor of the Duchy of Lancaster
Lord Chancellor
Lord Privy Seal
Master of the Rolls

and a few exalted people, such as:

the *Dalai Lama*, the *Aga Khan*. Also *God* and *the Prophet*.

3 Some titles serve as names, and therefore have initial capitals, though they also serve as descriptions: *the Archbishop of Canterbury, the Emir of Kuwait*. If you want to describe the office rather than the individual, use lower case: *The next archbishop of Canterbury will be a woman. Since the demise of the ninth duke, there has never been another duke of Portland.*

places Use upper case for definite geographical places, regions, areas and countries (*The Hague, Transylvania, Germany*), and for vague but recognised political or geographical areas (but *see* **Europe**, page 23):

Central, South, East and South-East Asia
the Gulf
East Asia (which is to be preferred to the Far East)
Highlands (of Scotland)
Middle East
Midlands (of England)
North Atlantic
North, Central and South America
South Atlantic
the West (as in the decline of the West)
West Country

Use capitals for particular buildings even if the name is not strictly accurate, eg, the *Foreign Office*.

And if in doubt use lower case (*the sunbelt*).

political terms

1 The full name of political parties is upper case, including the word party:

Communist (if a particular party)
Labour Party
Peasants' Party
Republican Party

2 But note that some parties do not have party as part of their names, so this should therefore be lower case:

Greece's *New Democracy party*
India's *Congress party*
Indonesia's *Golkar party*
Turkey's *Justice and Development party*

3 Note that usually only people are: *Democrats Christian Democrats Liberal Democrats* or *Social Democrats.*

Their parties, policies, candidates, committees, etc, are: *Democratic Christian Democratic Liberal Democratic* or *Social Democratic* (although a committee may be *Democrat-controlled*).

The exceptions are Britain's *Liberal Democrat Party* and Thailand's *Democrat Party.*

4 When referring to a specific party, write *Labour*, the *Republican nominee*, a prominent *Liberal*, etc, but use lower case in looser references to *liberals, conservatism, communists,* etc. *Tories*, however, are upper case, as is *New Labour.*

province, county, river, state, city Lower case when not strictly part of the name:

Cabanas province	New York state
Limpopo river	River Thames
Mississippi River	Washington state

trade names Use capitals:
Hoover Teflon Valium Walkman

miscellaneous (lower case)

19th amendment (but Article 19)
aborigines
amazon (female warrior)
angst
blacks
cabinet
civil servant
civil service
civil war (even America's)
cold war
common market
communist (generally)
constitution (even America's)
cruise missile
draconian
first world war
french windows
general synod
gentile
government
Gulf war
gypsy
internet
junior (as in George Bush junior)
Kyoto protocol
the left
mafia (any old group of criminals)
mecca (when used as a *mecca for tourists*)
new year (but New Year's Day)
Olympic games (and Asian, Commonwealth, European, etc)
opposition
philistine
platonic
the pope
the press
pyrrhic
the queen
quisling
realpolitik
revolution (everyone's)
the right
second world war
senior (as in George Bush senior)
six-day war
the shah
the speaker
state-of-the-union message
titanic
white paper
wild west
world wide web
young turk

miscellaneous (upper case)

Anglophone (but prefer English-speaking)
Antichrist
anti-Semitism
Atlanticist
the Bar
the Bible
Catholics
CD-ROM (should be set in small capitals)
Christ
Christmas Day
Christmas Eve
Coloureds (in South Africa)
the Cup Final
the Davis Cup
Earth (when, and only when, it is being discussed as a planet like Mars or Venus)

Francophone (but prefer
  French-speaking)
Hispanics
House of Laity
Koran
Labour Day
Mafia (the genuine article)
May Day
Mecca (in Saudi Arabia,
  California and Liberia)
Memorial Day
New Year's Day
New Year's Eve
Pershing missile (because it
  is named after somebody)
Protestants
Quartet (United States, EU,
  Russia, the UN)

the Queen's Speech
Russify
Semitic (-ism)
Social Security (in American
  contexts only, where it is
  used to mean pensions;
  what is usually understood
  by social security
  elsewhere is welfare in the
  United States)
Stealth fighter, bomber
Teamster
Ten Commandments
Test match
Utopia (-n)
Warsaw Pact

cartel A *cartel* is a group that restricts supply in order to drive up prices. Do not use it to describe any old syndicate or association of producers – especially of drugs.

case "There is perhaps no single word so freely resorted to as a trouble-saver," says Gowers, "and consequently responsible for so much flabby writing." Often you can do without it. *There are many cases of it being unnecessary* is better as *It is often unnecessary. If it is the case that* simply means *If. It is not the case* means *It is not so.*

Cassandra Do not use *Cassandra* just as a synonym for a prophet of doom. The most notable characteristic about her was that her predictions were always correct but never believed.

catalyst A *catalyst* is something that speeds up a chemical reaction while itself remaining unchanged. Do not confuse it with one of the agents.

Central Asian names *see* **names.**

centred on not *around* or *in.*

challenge Although duels and gauntlets have largely disappeared into history, modern life seems to consist of little else but *challenges*. At every turn, every president, every minister, every government, every business, everyone everywhere is faced with *challenges*. No one nowadays has to face a *change, difficulty, task* or *job*. Rather these are *challenges* – fiscal challenges, organisational challenges, structural challenges, regional challenges, demographic challenges, etc. Next time you grab the word *challenge*, drop it at once and think again.

charge If you *charge* intransitively, do so as a bull, cavalry officer or somesuch, not as an *accuser* (so avoid *The standard of writing was abysmal, he charged*).

charts and tables should, ideally, be understandable without reading the accompanying text. The main point of the heading should therefore be to assist understanding, though if it does so amusingly, so much the better. If the subject of the chart (or table) is unambiguous (because, say, it is in the middle of a story about Germany), the title need not reflect the subject. In that case, however, the subtitle should clearly state: *Number of occasions on which the word angst appears in German company reports, 2000-05.*

cherry-pick If you must use this cliché, note that *to cherry-pick means to engage in careful rather than indiscriminate selection*, whereas *a cherry-picker is a machine for raising pickers (and cleaners and so on) off the ground*.

Chinese is a language. It may be either *Mandarin* or *Cantonese*.

Chinese names *see* **names**.

circumstances stand around a thing, so it is *in*, not *under*, them.

civil society pops up a lot these days, often in the company of *citizenship skills, community leaders, good governance*, the *international community, social capital* and the like ("Development of civil society is social-reality specific" is a typical example). That should serve as a warning. It can, however, be a useful, albeit ill-defined term to describe collectively all non-commercial organisations between the family and the state. But do not use it as a euphemism for NGOs (non-governmental organisations), which is how it is usually employed.

clerical titles *see* **titles.**

clichés It would be quixotic to try to banish all clichés, and silly: a
phrase often becomes a cliché precisely because it does its job
rather well – at first. It is then copied so often and so unthinkingly
that the reader wearies of it, and groans. In his "A Dictionary of
Clichés" (1940), Eric Partridge wrote: "Clichés range from fly-
blown phrases (*much of a muchness; to all intents and purposes*),
metaphors that are now pointless (*lock, stock and barrel*), formulas
that have become mere counters (*far be it from me to...*) – through
sobriquets that have lost all their freshness and most of their
significance (*the Iron Duke*) – to quotations that are nauseating
(*cups that cheer but not inebriate*), and foreign phrases that are tags
(*longo intervallo, bête noire*)."

In truth, many of yesterday's clichés have become so much
a part of the language that they pass unnoticed; they are like
Orwell's dead metaphors. The ones most to be avoided are the
latest, the trendiest. Since they usually appeal to people who do
not have the energy to pick their own words, they are often found
in the wooden prose of bureaucrats, academics and businessmen,
though journalese is far from immune.

Can you speak the language of New Citizenship? asked an
advertisement placed by the British Home Office recently. It had
just set up a board to *"advise on ways in which existing language
and citizenship education resources and support services might
be developed"*, and was looking for a *"Vice Chair and 13 Board
members to help progress the challenging agenda that [lay] ahead"*.
The advertisement went on, not surprisingly, to mention *overall
strategic leadership, effective governance, a board fully focused
on delivery, a record of significant achievement in the Academic,
Education, Voluntary or Business Sectors, a keen interest in integration
and community cohesion, those experienced in social cohesion* and
the need for *strong interpersonal skills*.

A short article written by four European politicians for the
International Herald Tribune (July 3rd 2004) was in much the
same vein. It contained an *ambitious strategy, reform process,
send a message, momentum for structural economic reform back
on track, important impulse, significant challenges, immediate and
fundamental reforms, relocating operations, meet the competitiveness
challenge proactively, focus of reform efforts, social cohesion and
environmental sustainability, a number of key issues, innovative
(twice), latest knowledge, excessively burdensome rules, knowledge*

creation, concrete measures, industry-science networks, key to this goal, proactive course of action, at the end of the day, and so on. Perceptively, the authors added, *It is clear we have a lot of hard work to do. Difficult decisions will have to be made.*

("Political language is designed to ... give an appearance of solidity to pure wind." Orwell)

Clichés appear in lots of other contexts (*see also* **horrible words, journalese and slang, metaphors**). The following paragraphs may alert you to some of the commoner ones:

"At this moment in time, with all due respect, let me take this window of opportunity to share with you a few clichés that some people may find particularly irritating. Basically, I would have to begin by kick-starting the economy, on a level playing-field, of course, and then, going forward, I would want to give 110% to the creation of a global footprint before cherry-picking the co-workers to empower the underprivileged, motivate the on-train team and craft an exciting public space, not forgetting that, if the infrastructure is not to find itself between a rock and a hard place, at the end of the day, we shall have to get networking and engage in some blue-sky thinking to push the envelope way beyond even our usual out-of-the-box metrics."

"You see, unless you have vision and passion you will never grow the company. You won't even be able to trial your peers' road maps. You can talk the talk, but can you walk the walk? Can you commit to those parameters? Good. But right now it's time to draw a line in the sand and move on."

Nothing betrays the lazy writer faster than fly-blown phrases used in the belief that they are snappy, trendy or cool.

bridges too far	$64,000 questions
empires striking back	southern discomfort
kinder, gentler	back to the future
F-words	shaken, not stirred
flavours of the month	thirty-somethings
Generation X	windows of opportunity
hearts and minds	where's the beef?

These are usually from a film or television, or perhaps a politician. Others come into use less wittingly, often from social scientists. If you find yourself using any of the following vogue words, you should stop and ask yourself whether it is the best word for the job or if you would have used it in the same context five or ten years ago, and if not why not:

address, meaning *answer, deal with, attend to, look at*
care for and all caring expressions – how about *look after*?
commit to meaning *commit yourself to*
community (*see* page 36)
environment – in a writing environment you may want to make use of your correction fluid, rubber (or American eraser) or delete key
famously: usually redundant, nearly always irritating
focus: all the world's a stage, not a lens
historic: let historians, not contemporary commentators, be the judge
individual: fine as an adjective and occasionally as a noun, but increasingly favoured by the wooden-tongued as a longer synonym for *man, woman* or *person*
inform, when used as a pretentious alternative to *influence*
overseas – inexplicably, and often wrongly, used to mean *abroad* or *foreign*
participate in – use *take part in*, with more words but fewer syllables
process – a word properly applied to *attempts to bring about peace*, because they are meant to be evolutionary, but now often used in place of *talks*
relationship – *relations* can nearly always do the job
resources
skills
supportive – *helpful*?
transparency – *openness*?
wannabes

Such words should not be banned, but if you find yourself using them only because you hear others using them, not because they are the most appropriate ones in the context, you should avoid them. Overused words and off-the-shelf expressions make for stale prose.

coiffed not *coiffured.*

collapse (verb) is not transitive. You may collapse, but you may not collapse something.

colons *see* **punctuation**.

come up with Try *suggest, originate* or *produce.*

commas *see* **punctuation.**

commit Do not *commit to,* but by all means *commit yourself to* something.

community is a useful word in the context of religious or ethnic groups. But in many others it jars. Not only is it often unnecessary, it also purports to convey a sense of togetherness that may well not exist:

The *black community* means *blacks.*
The *business community* means *businessmen* (who are supposed to be competing, not colluding).
The *homosexual community* means *homosexuals* or *gays.*
The *intelligence community* means *spies.*
The *online community* means *geeks and nerds.*
The *migration and development communities* means NGOs.
The *international community,* if it means anything, means *other countries, aid agencies* or, just occasionally, *the family of nations.*
What the *global community* (*Financial Times,* July 12th 2005) means is a mystery.

Community is a word that crops up in the company of the meaningless jargon and vacuous expressions beloved of bombastic bureaucrats. Here is John Negroponte, appearing before the American Senate:

"Teamwork will remain my north star as director of national intelligence – not just for my immediate office but for the entire intelligence community. My objective will be to foster proactive co-operation ... The Office of Director of National Intelligence should be a catalyst for focusing on the hardest, most important questions ... Some argue that there are three intelligence communities ... a military intelligence community ... a foreign intelligence community ... and a domestic intelligence community ..."

company names Call companies by the names they call themselves. Here is a selection of names that are sometimes spelt incorrectly.

ABN AMRO	AstraZeneca
ACNeilsen	AT&T (American Telephone
Allied Domecq	and Telegraph)
AOL	

AXA, French insurance company
Barnes & Noble
Benetton
Berkshire Hathaway
Bertelsmann
BHP Billiton, South African/ Australian mining group
BNP Paribas
BP, which no longer refers to itself as British Petroleum
BSkyB
Cadbury Schweppes
Citigroup, Citibank in some countries
ConocoPhillips
DaimlerChrysler
DuPont
E.ON, German utility company
eBay
Eli Lilly
Ericcson, Swedish telecoms company
Exxon Mobil
GlaxoSmithKline

HBOS
Hewlett-Packard (HP)
JP Morgan Chase
Lehman Brothers
Merrill Lynch
Moody's, rating agency
News Corporation (News Corp)
Nomura Securities
Pfizer
Philip Morris
Philips, Dutch electronics multinational
Pillsbury
PricewaterhouseCoopers
Procter & Gamble
Sears, Roebuck
ThyssenKrupp
Vivendi Universal
Vodafone Group
Wal-Mart
Xstrata
Yahoo!
ZenithOptimedia

comparatives Take care. One thing may be *many times more expensive* than another. It cannot be *many times cheaper* (*The Economist*, August 9th 2003). Indeed, it can be cheaper only by proportion that is less than one. A different but similar mistake is to say that *Zimbabweans have grown twice as poor under his stewardship* (*The Economist*, April 9th 2005). Instead, say *Zimbabweans' incomes have fallen by half under his stewardship* (if that is what you mean, which, since it confuses income with wealth, it may not be).

compare A is compared *with* B when you draw attention to the difference. A is compared *to* B only when you want to stress their similarity.

Shall I compare thee to a summer's day?

compound the verb, does not mean *make worse*. It may mean *combine* or, intransitively, it may mean to *agree* or *come to terms*. To *compound a felony* means to *agree for a consideration not to prosecute*. (It is also used, with different senses, as a noun and adjective.)

comprise means *is composed of*. *The Democratic coalition comprises women, workers, blacks and Jews. Women make up* (not comprise) *three-fifths of the Democratic coalition*. Alternatively, *Three-fifths of the Democratic coalition is composed of women*.

confectionary is a sweet; *confectionery* is sweets in general.

contemporary *see* **current**.

continuous describes something uninterrupted. *Continual* admits of a break. If your neighbours play loud music every night, it is a *continual* nuisance; it is not a *continuous* one unless the music is never turned off.

contract *see* **subcontract**.

contrast, by or **in** *see* **by contrast, in contrast**.

convince Don't *convince* people *to* do something. In that context the word you want is *persuade*. *The prime minister was persuaded to call a June election; he was convinced of the wisdom of doing so only after he had won*.

coruscate means *sparkle* or *throw off flashes of light*, not *wither, devastate* or *reduce to wrinkles* (that's *corrugate*).

could is sometimes useful as a variant of *might*: *His coalition could* (or *might*) *collapse*. But take care. Does *He could call an election in May* mean *He might call an election in May* or *He would be allowed to call an election in May*?

countries and their inhabitants In most contexts favour simplicity over precision and use *Britain* rather than *Great Britain* or the *United Kingdom*, and *America* rather than the *United States*. ("In all pointed sentences, some degree of accuracy must be sacrificed to conciseness." Dr Johnson.)

Sometimes, however, it may be important to be precise. Remember therefore that *Great Britain* consists of *England, Scotland*

and *Wales*, which together with *Northern Ireland* (which we generally call *Ulster*, though Ulster strictly includes three counties in *Ireland*) make up the *United Kingdom*.

Holland, though a nice, short, familiar name, is strictly only two of the 11 provinces that make up *the Netherlands*, and the *Dutch* do not like the misuse of the shorter name. So use *the Netherlands*.

Ireland is simply *Ireland*. Although it is a republic, it is not the Republic of Ireland. Neither is it, in English, *Eire*.

Americans: Remember too that, although it is usually all right to talk about the inhabitants of the United States as *Americans*, the term also applies to everyone from Canada to Cape Horn. In a context where other North, Central or South American countries are mentioned, you should write *United States* rather than *America* or *American*, and it may even be necessary to write *United States citizens*.

USA and *US* are not to be used (if they were they would spatter the paper), except in charts and as part of an official name (eg, *US Steel*).

Do not use the names of capital cities as synonyms for their governments. *Britain will send a gunboat* is fine, but *London will send a gunboat* suggests that this will be the action of the people of London alone. To write *Washington and Moscow now differ only in their approach to Havana* is absurd.

EU should not be used without first spelling out the *European Union*. *Europe* and *Europeans* may sometimes be used as shorthand for citizens of countries of the European Union, but be careful: there are plenty of other Europeans too.

Scandinavia is primarily Norway and Sweden, but the term is often used to include Denmark, Iceland, Norway and Sweden, which, with Finland, make up the *Nordic countries*.

Madagascar: *Malagasy* is its adjective and the name of the inhabitants.

Note that a country is *it*, not she.

changes of name Where countries have made it clear that they wish to be called by a new (or an old) name, respect their requests. Thus:

Burkina Faso Côte d'Ivoire Myanmar Sri Lanka Thailand Zimbabwe

Zaire has now reverted to *Congo*. In contexts where

there can be no confusion with the ex-French country of
the same name, plain *Congo* will do. But if there is a risk of
misunderstanding, call it the *Democratic Republic of Congo*
(never DRC). The other Congo can be *Congo-Brazzaville* if
necssary. The river is now also the *Congo*. The people of either
country are also *Congolese*.

Former Soviet republics that are now independent
countries include:

Belarus (not *Belorus* or *Belorussia*), *Belarusian* (adjective)
Kazakhstan
Moldova (not *Moldavia*)
Tajikistan
Turkmenistan (see **Turk, Turkic, Turkmen, Turkoman** below)
Kyrgyzstan is the name of the country. Its adjective is
   Kyrgyzstani, which is also the name of one of its
   inhabitants. But *Kirgiz* is the noun and adjective of the
   language, and the adjective of Kirgiz people outside
   Kyrgyzstan. (*See also* **names**.)

Follow local practice when a country changes the names
of rivers, towns, etc, within it. Thus:

Almaty not *Alma Ata*
Chemnitz not *Karl-Marx-Stadt*
Chennai not *Madras*
Chernihiv not *Chernigov*
Chur not *Coire*
Kyiv not *Kiev*
Kolkata not *Calcutta*
Lviv not *Lvov*
Mumbai not *Bombay*
Nizhny Novgorod not *Gorky*
Papua not *Irian Jaya*
Polokwane not *Pietersburg*
Yangon not *Rangoon*
St Petersburg not *Leningrad*
Tshwane is the new name for the area round *Pretoria* but not
   yet for the city itself. (*See also* **placenames**.)

Turk, Turkic, Turkmen, Turkoman, etc

Turk, Turkish: noun and adjective of Turkey.
   Turkoman, Turkomans: member, members, of a branch

of the Turkish race mostly living in the region east of the Caspian sea once known as Turkestan and parts of Iran and Afghanistan; *Turkoman* may also be the language of the Turkmen – and an adjective.

Turkic: adjective applied to one of the branches of the Ural-Altaic family of languages – Uighur, Kazan Tatar, Kirgiz.

Turkmen: Turkoman or Turkomans living in Turkmenistan; adjective pertaining to them.

Turkmenistani: adjective of Turkmenistan; also a native of that country.

crescendo Not an acme, apogee, peak, summit or zenith but a *passage of increasing loudness*. You cannot therefore *build to a crescendo*.

crisis A decisive event or turning-point. Many of the economic and political troubles wrongly described as *crises* are really *persistent difficulties, sagas or affairs*.

critique is a noun. If you want a verb, try *criticise*.

currencies Use $ as the standard currency and, on first mention of sums in all other currencies except euros, give a dollar conversion in brackets.

Apart from those currencies that are written out in full (*see below*), write the abbreviation followed by the number.

Britain

pound, abbreviated as £
pence, abbreviated as *p*
1p, 2p, 3p, etc to *99p* (not £0.99)
£6 (not £6.00), £6.47
£5,000-6,000 (not £5,000-£6,000)
£5m-6m (not £5m-£6m)
£5 billion-6 billion (not £5-6 billion), £5.2 billion-6.2 billion

America

dollar, abbreviated as $, will do generally; *US$* if there is a mixture of dollar currencies (*see below*)
cents, abbreviated as *c*; but spell out, unless part of a larger number: $4.99

other dollar currencies

A$	Australian dollars	NT$	Taiwanese dollars
C$	Canadian dollars	NZ$	New Zealand dollars
HK$	Hong Kong dollars	S$	Singaporean dollars
M$	Malaysian dollars		

Europe

euro, plural *euros*, abbreviated as €, for those countries that have adopted it.

cents, abbreviated as *c*: spell out, unless part of a larger number.

Write the abbreviation followed by the figure: €100 (not 100 euros).

DM, BFr, drachmas, FFr, Italian lire, IR£ (punts), *markkas, Asch, Ptas* and other currencies of the euro area have all been replaced by €, but may turn up in historical references.

DKr Danish krone (plural *kroner*)

NKr Norwegian krone (*kroner*)

SFr Swiss franc, SFr1m (not *1m Swiss francs*)

SKr Swedish krona (plural *kronor*)

sums in all other currencies are written in full, with the number first.

Brazil, *real*	100m *reais* (see below)
China, yuan	100m yuan (not renminbi) (see below)
India, rupee	100m rupees
Nigeria, naira	100m naira
peso currencies	100m pesos
South Africa, rand	100m rand (not rands)
Turkey, Turkish lira	100m liras
But Japan, yen	¥, ¥1,000 (not 1,000 *yen*)

Brazil Because of the risk of confusion with its English homonym, the *real* (plural *reais*) – but no other currency – is italicised in all text.

China Properly, Chinese sums are expressed as, eg, 1 yuan RMB, meaning 1 yuan renminbi. *Yuan*, which means *money*, is the Chinese unit of currency. *Renminbi*, which means the *people's currency*, is the description of the yuan, as sterling is the description of the pound. Use *yuan*.

See also **figures**; and **currencies** and **measures** in Part 3.

current, contemporary *Current* and *contemporary* mean *at that time*, not necessarily *at this time*. So a series of current prices from 1960 to 1970 will not be in *today's prices*, just as *contemporary art* in 1800 was not *modern art*. *Contemporary history* is a contradiction in terms.

cusp is a pointed end or a horn of, for example, the moon, or the point at which two branches of a curve meet. So it is odd to write, say, "Japan is on the cusp of a recovery" unless you think that recovery is about to end.

cyber-expressions Most cyber-terms are lower case: *cyber-attack*, *cyber-soccer*, etc, but *cybernetics*, *cyberspace* and *cyberwars*.

dashes *see* **punctuation**.

dates month, day, year, in that order, with no commas:

July 5th	1996-99
Monday July 5th	2002-05
July 5th 2005	1998-2003
July 27th-August 3rd 2005	1990s
July 2002	

Do not write *on June 10th-14th*; prefer between *June 10th and 14th*. If, say, ministers are to meet over two days, write *on December 14th and 15th*.

Do not burden the reader with dates of no significance, but give a date rather than just *last week*, which can cause confusion. *This week* and *next week* are permissible.

Dates are often crucial to an account of events, but sentences (and, even more, articles) that begin with a date can be clumsy and off-putting. *This week Congress is due to consider the matter* is often better put as *Congress is due to consider the matter this week*. The effect is even more numbing if a comma is inserted: *This week, Congress is due to consider the matter*, though this construction is sometimes merited when emphasis is needed on the date.

deal (verb) Transitively, *deal* means distribute: "He was dealt two aces, two kings and a six." Intransitively, *deal* means *engage in business*. Do not *deal* drugs, horses, weapons, etc; *deal in* them.

decimate means to destroy a proportion (originally a tenth) of a group of people or things, not to destroy them all or nearly all.

demographics No, the word is *demography*.

deprecate, depreciate To *deprecate* is to *argue* or *plead against* (by prayer or otherwise). To *depreciate* is to *lower in value*.

different from not *to* or *than.*

dilemma Not just any old awkwardness but one with horns, being, properly, a form of argument (the horned syllogism) in which you find yourself committed to accept one of two propositions each of which contradicts your original contention. Thus a *dilemma* offers the choice between two alternatives, each with equally nasty consequences.

discreet, discrete *Discreet means circumspect or prudent. Discrete means separate or distinct.* Remember that *"Questions are never indiscreet. Answers sometimes are."* (Oscar Wilde)

disinterested means *impartial; uninterested means bored.* "*Disinterested curiosity is the lifeblood of civilisation."* (G.M. Trevelyan)

Dominicans Take care. Do they come from Dominica? Or the Dominican Republic? Or are they friars?

down to earth yes, but *Occasional court victories are not down to human rights (The Economist).* No: *down to* does not mean *attributable to, the responsibility of* or even *up to (It's up to you).*

due process is a technical term, or piece of **jargon**, which was first used in England in 1355. It comes in two forms, *substantive due process*, which relates to the duties of governments to act rationally and proportionally when doing anything that affects citizens' rights, and *procedural due process*, which relates to the need for fair procedures. If you use the expression, make sure it is clear what you mean by it.

due to when used to mean *caused by* must follow a noun, as in *The cancellation, due to rain, of ...* Do not write *It was cancelled due to rain.* If you mean *because of* and for some reason are reluctant to say it, you probably want *owing to. It was cancelled owing to rain* is all right.

Dutch names *see* **names.**

earnings Do not write *earnings* when you mean *profits* (try to say if they are *operating, gross, pre-tax* or *net*).

-ee *employees, evacuees, detainees, divorcee, referees, refugees* but, please, no *attendees* (those attending), *draftees* (conscripts), *enrollees* (participants), *escapees* (escapers), *indictees* (the indicted), *retirees* (the retired), or *standees*. A *divorcee* may be male or female.

e-expressions Except at the start of a sentence, the *e-* is lower case and hyphenated:

e-business
e-commerce
e-mail

When giving *websites*, do not include *http://*. Just *www* is enough: *www.economist.com*
Computer terms are also usually lower case:

dotcom
home-page
laptop
online
the net (and internet)
the web, website and world wide web

See also **cyber-expressions**.

effect the verb, means to *accomplish*, so *The novel effected a change in his attitude*. *See also* **affect**.

-effective, -efficient *Cost-effective* sounds authoritative, but does it mean *good value for money, gives a big bang for the buck* or just plain *cheap*? If *cheap*, say *cheap*. *Energy-efficient* is also dubious. Does it mean *thrifty, economical* or something else? *Efficiency* is the ratio of energy put out to energy put in.

effectively, in effect *Effectively* means *with effect*; if you mean *in effect*, say it. *The matter was effectively dealt with on Friday* means it was done well on Friday. *The matter was, in effect, dealt with on Friday* means it was *more or less attended to* on Friday. *Effectively leaderless* would do as a description of the demonstrators in East Germany in 1989 but not those in Tiananmen Square, also in 1989. The devaluation of the Slovak currency in 1993, described by some as *an effective 8%*, turned out to be a rather ineffective 8%.

either ... or *see* **none.**

elections *see* **grammar and syntax.**

enclave, exclave An *enclave* is a piece of territory or territorial water entirely surrounded by foreign territory (Ceuta, Kaliningrad, Melilla, Nagorno-Karabakh, Nakhichevan). An *exclave* is the same thing, viewed differently, if, and only if, it belongs to another country (so Andorra and San Marino are not exclaves).

enormity means a *crime, sin* or *monstrous wickedness*. It does not mean *immensity*.

environment is often unavoidable, but it's not a pretty word. Avoid *the business environment, the school environment, the work environment*, etc. Try to rephrase the sentence – *conditions for business, at school, at work*, etc. *Surroundings* can sometimes do the job.

epicentre means *that point on the earth's surface above the centre of an earthquake*. To say that *Mr Putin was at the epicentre of the dispute* suggests that the argument took place underground.
     The *hypocentre*, incidentally, is *the place on the surface of the earth below an explosion* (which at Hiroshima in 1945, for example, was 580 metres above the ground). It is the same as *ground zero*.

eponymous is the adjective of *eponym*, which is *the person or thing after which something is named*. So George Canning was the *eponymous hero* of the Canning Club, Hellen was the *eponymous ancestor* of the Hellenes (Greeks), Ninus was the *eponymous founder* of Nineveh. Do not say *John Sainsbury, the founder of the eponymous supermarket*. Rather he was the *eponymous founder of J. Sainsbury's*.

ethnic groups Your first concern should be to avoid giving offence. But also avoid mealy-mouthed **euphemisms** and terms that have not generally caught on despite promotion by pressure-groups. *Ethnic* meaning *concerning nations or races,* or even something ill-defined in between, is a useful word. But do not be shy of *race* and *racial.* After several years in which *race* was seen as a purely social concept, not a scientific one, the term is coming back among scientists as a shorthand way of speaking about genetic rather than cultural or political differences. *See also* **political correctness.**

Anglo-Saxon is not a synonym for *English-speaking.* Neither the United States nor Australia is an Anglo-Saxon country; nor is Britain. Anglo-Saxon capitalism does not exist.

Asians In Britain, but nowhere else, *Asians* is often used to mean *immigrants and their descendants from the Indian subcontinent.* Many such people are coming to dislike the term, and many foreigners must assume it means people from all over Asia, so take care. Note that, even in the usage peculiar to Britain, *Asian* is not synonymous with *Muslim.*

blacks In many countries, including the United States, many black people are happy to be called *blacks,* although some prefer to be *African-Americans. Black* is shorter and more straightforward, but use either.

mixed race Do not call people who are neither pure white nor pure black *browns.* People of mixed race in South Africa are *Coloureds.*

other groups The inhabitants of *Azerbaijan* are *Azerbaijanis,* some of whom, but not all, are *Azeris.* Those *Azeris* who live in other places, such as Iran, are not *Azerbaijanis.* Similarly, many Croats are not Croatian, many Serbs not Serbian, many Uzbeks not Uzbekistanis, etc.

Spanish-speakers in the US When writing about Spanish-speaking people in the United States, use either *Latino* or *Hispanic* as a general term, but try to be specific (eg, Mexican-American). Many Latin Americans (eg, those from Brazil) are not Hispanic.

euphemisms Avoid, where possible, euphemisms and
circumlocutions, especially those promoted by interest-groups
keen to please their clients or organisations anxious to avoid
embarrassment. This does not mean that good writers should
be insensitive of giving offence: on the contrary, if you are to be
persuasive, you would do well to be courteous. But a good writer
owes something to plain speech, the English language and the
truth, as well as to manners. **Political correctness** can be carried
too far.

So, in most contexts, *offending* behaviour is probably *criminal*
behaviour. *Female teenagers* are *girls*, not *women*. *Living with
mobility impairment* probably means *wheelchair-bound*. *Developing*
countries are often *stagnating* or even *regressing* (try *poor*)
countries. The *underprivileged* may be *disadvantaged*, but are more
likely just *poor* (the very concept of *underprivilege* is absurd, since
it implies that some people receive less than their fair share of
something that is by definition an advantage or prerogative).

Enron's *document-management* policy simply meant *shredding*.
The Pentagon's practice of *enhanced interrogation* is *torture*, just
as its practice of *rendition* is probably *torture contracted out to
foreigners*. France's proposed *solidarity contribution* on airline
tickets is a *tax*. The British solicitor-general's *evidential deficiency*
is *no evidence*, and George Bush's *reputational problem* just means
he is *mistrusted*. It is sometimes useful to talk of *human-rights
abuses* but often the sentence can be rephrased more pithily and
accurately. *The army is accused of committing numerous human-
rights abuses* probably means *The army is accused of torture
and murder*. *Decommissioning weapons* means *disarming*. *Being
economical with the truth* famously means *lying*. *A high net-worth
individual* is a *rich man* or *rich woman*. *Zero-percent financing* means
an *interest-free loan*.

See also **affirmative action**.

Euro-terms *see* **capitals**.

ex- (and former) Be careful. A *Labour Party ex-member* has lost his
seat; an *ex-Labour member* has lost his party.

execute means *put to death by law*. Do not use it as a synonym for
murder. An *extra-judicial execution* is a contradiction in terms.

fact *The fact that* can often be reduced to *that*.

factoid A *factoid* is something that sounds like a fact, is thought by many to be a fact (perhaps because it is repeated so often), but is not in fact a fact.

federalist in Britain, someone who believes in centralising the powers of associated states; in the United States and Europe, someone who believes in decentralising them.

fellow Often unnecessary, especially before *countrymen* ("Friends, Romans, *fellow-countrymen*"?).

fewer than, less than *Fewer* (not *less*) *than seven speeches, fewer than seven samurai.* Use *fewer*, not *less*, with numbers of individual items or people. *Less than £200, less than 700 tonnes of oil, less than a third*, because these are measured quantities or proportions, not individual items.

fief not *fiefdom*.

figures Never start a sentence with a figure; write the number in words instead.

Use words for simple numerals from one to ten inclusive, except: in references to pages; in percentages (eg, 4%); and in sets of numerals, some of which are higher than ten.

Deaths from this cause in the past three years were 14, 9 and 6.

Always use numbers with units of measurement, even for those less than ten:

4 metres, but *four cows*

It is occasionally permissible to use words rather than numbers when referring to a rough or rhetorical figure (such as *a thousand curses, a hundred years of solitude).*

In all other cases, though, use figures for numerals from 11 upwards.

first to tenth centuries, the 11th century   a 29-year-old man
20th century, 21st century   a man in his 20s
20th-century ideas   20th anniversary
in 100 years' time

The *Thirty Years War* is an exception.

decimal point Use figures for all numerals that include a decimal point (eg, 4.25).

fractions Figures may be appropriate for fractions, if the context is either technical or precise, or both:

Though the poll's figures were supposed to be accurate to within 1%, his lead of 4¹/₄ points turned out on election day to be minus 3¹/₂.

Where precision is less important but it is nonetheless impossible to shoot off the fraction, words may look better:

Though the beast was sold as two-year-old, it turned out to be two-and-a-half times that.

Fractions should be hyphenated (one-half, three-quarters, etc) and, unless they are attached to whole numbers (8¹/₂, 29³/₄), spelled out in words, even when the figures are higher than ten:

He gave a tenth of his salary to the church, a twentieth to his mistress and a thirtieth to his wife.

fractions and decimals Do not compare a fraction with a decimal. So avoid:

The rate fell from 3¹/₄% to 3.1%.

Fractions are more precise than decimals (3.33 neglects an infinity of figures that are embraced by ¹/₃), but your readers probably do not think so. You should therefore use fractions for rough figures:

Kenya's population is growing at 3¹/₂% a year, A hectare is 2¹/₂ acres and decimals for more exact ones:

The retail price index is rising at an annual rate of 10.6%.

But treat all numbers with respect. That usually means resisting the precision of more than one decimal place, and generally favouring rounding off. Beware of phoney over-precision.

hyphens and figures Do not use a hyphen in place of *to* except with figures:

He received a sentence of 15-20 years in jail but *He promised to have escaped within three to four weeks.*

Latin usage It is outdated to use Latin words. So, with figures, do not write *per caput, per capita* or *per annum*. Use:

a head or *per head*
a person or *per person*
a year or *per year*
2 litres of water per person
prices rose by 10% a year

See also **per caput**.

measurements Since Britain has gone over to the metric system, in most non-American contexts prefer:

hectares to acres
kilometres (or *km*) to miles
metres to yards
litres to gallons
kilos (*kg*) to lb
tonnes to tons
Celsius to Fahrenheit, etc

k, m and *M* are standard international metric abbreviations for thousand, thousandth and million.

1   In American contexts, you may use the measurements more familiar to Americans (though remember that American pints, quarts, gallons, etc, are smaller than imperial ones).

Regardless of which you choose, you should give an equivalent, on first use, in the other units:

It was hoped that after improvements to the engine the car would give 20km to the litre (47 miles per American gallon), compared with its present average of 15km per litre.

2   Petrol Remember that in only a few countries do you now buy petrol in imperial gallons. In America it is sold in American gallons; in most other places it is sold in litres.

3   Note that a four-by-four vehicle can be a 4×4.

million, billion, trillion, quadrillion Use *m* for million. Spell out billion and trillion (though their conventional abbreviations are *bn* and *trn*).

8m   8 billion
£8m   €8 billion

A *billion* is a thousand million, a *trillion* a thousand billion. (A *quadrillion* is a thousand trillion.)

per cent, percentage points
Use the sign % instead of per cent. But write *percentage*, never *%age* (though in most contexts *proportion* or *share* is preferable).
A fall from 4% to 2% is a drop of two percentage points, or of 50%, but not of 2%. (*See also* **per cent.**)

ranges Write:

5,000-6,000
5-6%
5m-6m (*not* 5-6m)
5 billion-6 billion

But:

Sales rose from 5m to 6m (not 5m-6m); estimates ranged between 5m and 6m (not 5m-6m).

ratios Where *to* is being used as part of a ratio, it is usually best to spell it out.

They decided, by nine votes to two, to put the matter to the general assembly which voted, 27 to 19, to insist that the ratio of vodka to tomato juice in a bloody mary should be at least one to three, though the odds of this being so in most bars were put at no better than 11 to 4.

Where a ratio is being used adjectivally, figures and hyphens may be used, but only if one of the figures is greater than ten:

a 50-20 vote
a 19-9 vote

Otherwise, spell out the figures and use *to*:

a two-to-one vote
a ten-to-one probability

finally Do not use *finally* when you mean *at last*. *Richard Burton finally marries Liz Taylor* would have been all right second time round but not first.

firm Accountants', consultants', lawyers' and other partnerships are *firms*, not *companies*. Huge enterprises, like GE, GM, Ford, Microsoft and so on, should, by contrast, normally be called *companies*, although such outfits can sometimes be called *firms* for variety.

flaunt, flout *Flaunt* means display; *flout* means disdain. If you *flout* this distinction, you will *flaunt* your ignorance.

focus can be a useful word. It is shorter than *concentrate* and sharper than *look at*. But it is overused (*see* page 35).

footnotes, sources, references *see* **footnotes, sources, references** in Part 3.

foreign languages and translation Occasionally, a foreign language may provide the *mot juste*. But try not to use foreign words and phrases unless there is no English alternative, which is unusual. So:

a year or *per year*, not *per annum*
a person or *per person*, not *per caput* or *per capita*
beyond one's authority, not *ultra vires*
(*See also* **italics**.)

names of foreign companies, institutions, groups, parties, etc Do not translate, or italicise, the name of a foreign company, institution or organisation even if it is, or includes, an ordinary word with an English equivalent. So:

Forza Italia
Médecins Sans Frontières
the Parti Québécois in Canada
yakuza (not 8-9-3)

Note that if an abbreviation is also given, that may be the initials of the foreign name:

UMP for France's *Union for a Presidential Majority*
SPD for the *Social Democratic Party of Germany*
PAN for *Mexico's National Action Party*

But some should be translated:

Italy's *Olive Tree* (not *Ulivo*)
the German *Christian Democratic Union* (not the *Christlich Demokratische Union*)
the *Shining Path* (not *Sendero Luminoso*)
the *National Assembly* (not the *Assemblée Nationale*)

placenames Some placenames are better translated if they are well known in English:

St Mark's Square in Venice (not *Piazza San Marco*)
the French *Elysée Palace* (not the *Palais de l'Elysée*)

titles of foreign books, films, etc The titles of foreign books, films, plays, operas and TV programmes present difficulties. Some are so well known that they are unlikely to need translation:

"*Das Kapital*" "*Mein Kampf*" "*Le Petit Prince*" "*Die Fledermaus*"

And sometimes the meaning of the title may be unimportant in the context, so a translation is not necessary:

"*Hiroshima, Mon Amour*"

But often the title will be significant, and you will want to translate it. One solution, easy with classics, is simply to give the English translation:

"*One Hundred Years of Solitude*" "*The Leopard*" "*War and Peace*" "*The Tin Drum*"

This is usually the best practice to follow with pamphlets, articles and non-fiction, too.

But sometimes, especially with books and films that are little known among English-speakers or unobtainable in English (perhaps you are reviewing one), you may want to give both the original title and a translation, thus:

"11 *Septembre 2001: l'Effroyable Imposture*" ("*September 11th 2001: the Appalling Deception*")
"*La Règle du Jeu*" ("*The Rules of the Game*")
"*La Traviata*" ("*The Sinner*")

Such titles do not follow the rule of italicising for foreign words. Treat them as if they were in English.

Note that book publishers follow different rules here. (*See* **italics.**)

translating words and phrases If you want to translate a foreign word or phrase, even if it is the name of a group or newspaper or party, just put it in brackets without inverted commas, so:

Arbeit macht frei (*work makes free*)
jihad (*struggle*)
Médecins Sans Frontières (*Doctors Without Borders*)
Pravda (*Truth*)
zapatero (*shoemaker*)

forensic means *pertaining to courts of law* (held by the Romans in the forum) or, more loosely, *the application of science to legal issues. Forensic medicine is medical jurisprudence.*

forgo, forego *Forgo* means do without; it forgoes the e. *Forego* means go before. A *foregone conclusion* is one that is predetermined; a *forgone conclusion* is non-existent.

former *see* **ex-.**

former and latter Avoid the use of *the former* and *the latter* whenever possible. It usually causes confusion.

Frankenstein was not the monster, but its creator.

free is an adjective or an adverb (and also a transitive verb), so you cannot have or do anything *for free.* Either you have it *free* or you have it *for nothing.*

French names *see* **names**.

fresh is not a synonym for *new* or *more*. *A few hundred fresh bodies are being recovered every day*, reported *The Economist* improbably, two months after a tsunami had struck. Use with care.

full stops *see* **punctuation**.

fulsome is an old word that Americans generally use only to mean *cloying, insincere* or *excessively flattering*. In British English it can also mean *copious, abundant* or *lavish*.

fund (verb) is a technical term, meaning to convert floating debt into more or less permanent debt at fixed interest. Try to avoid it if you mean to *finance* or to *pay for*.

garner means *store*, not *gather*.

gearing is an ugly word which, if used, needs to be explained. It may be either the *ratio of debt to equity* or the *ratio of debt to total capital employed*. (*See also* **leverage**.)

gender is nowadays used in several ways. One is common in feminist writing, where the term has a technical meaning. "One is not born a woman, one becomes one," argued Simone de Beauvoir: in other words, one chooses one's gender. In such a context it would be absurd to use the word *sex*; the term must be *gender*. But, in using it thus, try to explain what you mean by it. Even feminists do not agree on a definition.

   The primary use of *gender*, though, is in grammar, where it is applied to words, not people. If someone is female, that is her *sex*, not her *gender*. (The gender of *Mädchen*, the German word for girl, is neuter, as is *Weib*, a wife or woman.) So do not use *gender* as a synonym for *sex*. *Gender studies* probably means *feminism*.

generation Take care. You can be a second-generation Frenchman, but if you are a second-generation immigrant it means you have left the country your parents came to.

gentlemen's agreement not *gentleman's*.

German names *see* **names**.

get is an adaptable verb, but it has its limits. A man does not *get* sacked or promoted, he *is* sacked or promoted. Nor does a prize-winner *get to* shake hands with the president, or spend the money all at once; he *gets the chance to*, is *able to*, or *allowed to*.

global Globalisation can go to the head. It is not necessary to describe, eg, the head of Baker & Mackenzie as the *global head* of that firm.

And what is a *global vacancy* (as advertised by The Economist Group)?

good in parts is what the curate said about an egg that was wholly bad. He was trying to be polite.

gourmet, gourmand *Gourmet* means *epicure*; *gourmand* means *greedy-guts*.

governance *Corporate governance* has now entered the language as a useful, albeit ugly and ill-defined, term to describe the rules relating to the conduct of business. The popularity of *governance* in other contexts is more difficult to understand. An old word, it had largely fallen into suitable disuse until Harold Wilson chose it in 1976 for the title of his memoirs ("The Governance of Britain"), presumably to dignify an undistinguished prime ministership. It means simply *government*, a word that serves the same purpose without any of the pretensions or pomposity of *governance*.

grammar and syntax Try not to be sloppy in the construction of your sentences and paragraphs. A single issue of *The Economist* contained the following:

When closed at night, the fear is that this would shut off rather than open up part of the city centre. Unlike Canary Wharf, the public will be able to go to the top to look out over the city. Only a couple of months ago, after an unbroken string of successes in state and local elections, pollsters said ...

Some hints are provided here on avoiding pitfalls, infelicities and mistakes; this is not a comprehensive guide to English grammar and syntax.

a or the Remember that *Barclays* is a *British bank*, not *the British bank*, just as *Ford* is *a car company*, not *the car company*, and *Luciano Pavarotti* is *an opera singer*, not *the opera singer*. If it seems absurd to describe someone or something thus – that is, with the indefinite article – you can probably dispense with the description altogether or insert an extra word or two that may be useful to the reader: *Ford, America's second-biggest car company.*

adjectives and adverbs Adjectives qualify nouns, adverbs modify

verbs. If you have a sentence that contains the words *firstly,
secondly, more importantly*, etc, they almost certainly ought to
be *first, second, more important*.

adjectives of proper nouns If proper nouns have adjectives, use
them.

> *Crimean war* (not the Crimea war)
> *Dutch East India Company* (not the Holland East India
>   Company)
> *Lebanese* (not Lebanon) *civil war*
> *Mexican* (not Mexico) *problem*
> *Pakistani* (not Pakistan) *government*
> *Scottish Office* (not the Scotland Office)

It is permissible to use the noun as an adjective if to do
otherwise would cause confusion.

An *African initiative* suggests the proposal came *from
Africa*, whereas an *Africa initiative* suggests it was *about Africa*.

Californian, Texan Do not feel you have to follow American
convention in using words like *Californian* and *Texan*
only as nouns. In British English, it is quite acceptable to
write a *Californian* (not *California*) *judge*, *Texan* (not *Texas*)
scandal, etc.

> "*Mr Gedge ... was not fond of St Rocque, and this morning
> it would have seemed less attractive to him than ever, for
> three of his letters bore Californian postmarks and their
> contents had aggravated the fever of his home-sickness.*"
> (P.G. Wodehouse, "Hot Water")
> "The local avant-garde was in one of its 'painting is dead'
> phases, and was automatically dismissive of things
> Californian anyway." (Peter Schjeldahl, *The New Yorker*,
> May 9th 2005)

collective nouns – singular or plural? There is no firm rule about
the number of a verb governed by a singular collective noun.
It is best to go by the sense – that is, whether the collective
noun stands for a single entity:

> The council was elected in March.
> The me generation has run its course.
> The staff is loyal.

or for its constituents:

The council are at sixes and sevens.
The preceding generation are all dead.
The staff are at each other's throats.

Do not, in any event, slavishly give all singular collective nouns singular verbs: *The couple are now living apart* is preferable to *The couple is now living apart.*

pair and couple Treat both a *pair* and a *couple* as plural.

majority When it is used in an abstract sense, it takes the singular; when it is used to denote the elements making up the majority, it should be plural.

A two-thirds majority is needed to amend the constitution but *A majority of the Senate were opposed.*

number Rule: *The number is ...; A number are ...*

comparisons Take care, too, when making comparisons, to compare like with like:

The Belgian economy is bigger than Russia should be *Belgium's economy is bigger than Russia's.*

An advertisement for *The Economist* recently declared,

Our style and our whole philosophy are different from other publications.

contractions Don't overdo the use of *don't, isn't, can't, won't,* etc.

false possessive Avoid the false possessive: *London's Heathrow Airport.*

genitive Take care with the genitive. It is fine to say a *friend of Bill's,* just as you would say *a friend of mine,* so you can also say *a friend of Bill's and Carol's.* But it is also fine to say a *friend of Bill,* or *a friend of Bill and Carol.* What you must not say is *Bill and Carol's friend.* If you wish to use that construction, you must say *Bill's and Carol's friend,* which is cumbersome.

gerunds Respect the gerund. Gerunds look like participles
– *running, jumping, standing* – but are more noun-like, and
should never therefore be preceded by a personal pronoun.
So the following are wrong: *I was awoken by him snoring, He
could not prevent them drowning, Please forgive me coming late.*

Those sentences should have ended:

his snoring, their drowning, my coming late.

In other words, use the possessive adjective rather than
the personal pronoun.

indirect speech If you use indirect speech in the past tense, you
must change the tense of the speaker's words appropriately:

*Before he died, he said, "I abhor the laziness that is commonplace
nowadays"* becomes *Before he died, he said he abhorred the
laziness that was commonplace nowadays.*

nouns acting as verbs Do not force nouns or other parts of
speech to act as verbs: *A woman who was severely brain-
damaged in 1990* would be better put as *A woman whose brain
was severely damaged in 1990* (unless, remarkably, she was no
longer brain-damaged at some later date).

participle Do not use a participle unless you make it clear what it
applies to. Here are some examples of confused construction:

*Proceeding along this line of thought, the cause of the train crash
becomes clear.*

*Looking out from the city's tallest building, the houses stretch for
miles and miles.*

It is hard to beat this statement by a "retired public relations/
communications practitioner" standing for election as a trustee
of the Royal Society of Arts:

*"Committed to invigorating perspectives in pursuit of the
manifesto, and assisted by an active Scottish committee,
programme diversity is deepening Scottish engagement across a
wider range of more visible joint partner and sponsorship-assisted
events."*

passive or active? Be direct. Use the active tense. *A hit B* describes the event more concisely than *B was hit by A*.

plural nouns

1   The *-ics* words on page 65 (Abstract nouns) are plural when preceded by *the*, or *the* plus an adjective, or with a possessive. For example:

The politics of Afghanistan have a logic all their own.
The dynamics of the dynasty were dynamite.
The economics of publishing are uncertain.
The athletics will take place in London.

2   These are plural:

antics	histrionics
atmospherics	hysterics
basics	tactics
graphics	statistics

Specifics are discouraged (try *details*), as are **demographics.**

3   *Data* and *media* are plural. So are *whereabouts*.

4   *Elections* are not always plural. If, as in the United States, several votes (for the presidency, the Senate, the House of Representatives, etc) are held on the same day, it is correct to talk about *elections*. But in, say, Britain parliamentary polls are usually held on their own, in a single *general election.*

    The *opposition demanded an election* is often preferable to *The opposition demanded fresh elections.* And to write *The next presidential elections are due in 2010* suggests there will be more than one presidential poll in that year.

    Make sure that plural nouns have plural verbs. Too often, in the pages of *The Economist*, they do not.
Kogalym today is one of the few Siberian oil towns which are [not is] *almost habitable.*
What better evidence that snobbery and elitism still hold [not holds] *back ordinary British people?* – and this in a leader on education.

quoting If you wish to quote someone, either give a date or use the present tense:

"He leaves a legacy of wisdom," said John Smith the next day or *... says Mr John Smith.*

The following paragraph is all too typical:

What next for Mistekistan? This week an uneasy peace broke out on the streets of Erati, the capital, after angry crowds besieged the palace of President Iyas Abikhernozthanayev. The president, who was head of the local communist party when Mistekistan was a Soviet republic called Sumistekia, fled to neighbouring Flyspekistan, where he was seeking asylum. However, fighting broke out between the Dabtchiks and the Bifsteks, two minorities in the south. The president of nearby Itznojokistan might try to broker a peace. "It looks a mess," said Professor Eniole Kwote of Meganostril University, whose centre for autocratic studies recently published a study saying the entire region is a shambles.

It would be better as:

What next for Mistekistan? An uneasy peace broke out this week on the streets of Erati, the capital, after angry crowds had besieged the palace of President Iyas Abikhernozthanayev. The president, who had been head of the local communist party when Mistekistan was a Soviet republic called Sumistekia, has fled to neighbouring Flyspekistan, where he is seeking asylum. However, fighting has broken out between Dabtchiks and Bifsteks, two minorities in the south. The president of nearby Itznojokistan may try to broker a peace. "It looks a mess," says Professor Eniole Kwote of Meganostril University, whose centre for autocratic studies recently published a study saying the entire region was a shambles.

singular nouns

1   A *government*, a *party*, a *company* (whether Tesco or Marks and Spencer) and a *partnership* (Skidmore, Owings & Merrill) are all *it* and take a singular verb.

2   *Brokers* are singular.

Legg Mason Wood Walk is preparing a statement.

So avoid:

stockbrokers *Furman Selz Mager*, bankers *Chase Manhattan* or accountants *Ernst & Young*.

3   *Chemical, drug, pension*: prefer the singular when referring to:

chemical (not *chemicals*) *companies*
drug- (not *drugs*) *traffickers*
pension (not *pensions*) *systems*

4   Countries are singular, even if their names look plural.

The Philippines has a congressional system, as does the United States; the Netherlands does not.

   The *United Nations* is also singular.

5   Abstract nouns that look plural:

acoustics	mathematics
athletics	mechanics
ballistics	physics
dynamics	politics
economics	propaganda
kinetics	statics

when being used generally, without the definite article, are singular. For example:

Economics is the dismal science.
Politics is the art of the possible (Bismarck).
Statics is a branch of physics.

6   Some games are singular:

billiards	darts
bowls	fives

   But teams that take the name of a town, country or university are plural, even when they look singular:

England were bowled out for 56.

7   *Law and order* defies the rules of grammar and is singular.

split infinitives Happy the man who has never been told that it is wrong to split an infinitive: the ban is pointless. Unfortunately, to see the rule broken is so annoying to so many people that you should observe it.

subjunctive Use the subjunctive properly. If you are posing a hypothesis contrary to fact, you must use the subjunctive. *If I were you ...* or *If Hitler were alive today, he could tell us whether he kept a diary.*

If the hypothesis may or may not be true, you do not use the subjunctive. *If this diary is not Hitler's, we shall be glad we did not publish it.*

If you have *would* in the main clause, you must use the subjunctive in the *if* clause. *If you were to disregard this rule, you would make a fool of yourself.*

It is common nowadays to use the subjunctive in such constructions as:

He demanded that the Russians withdraw, They insisted that the Americans also move back, The referee suggested both sides cool it, In soccer it is necessary that everyone remain civil.

This construction is correct, and has always been used in America, whence it has recrossed the Atlantic. In Britain, though, it fell into disuse some time ago except in more formal contexts:

I command the prisoner be summoned, I beg that the motion be put to the house.

In British English, but not in American, another course would be to insert the word *should*:

He demanded that the Russians should withdraw, The Americans should also move back, Both sides should cool it, Everyone should remain civil.

Alternatively, some of the sentences could be rephrased:

He asked the Russians to withdraw, It is necessary for everyone to remain civil.

See also **may and might**.

tenses Any account of events that have taken place must use a past tense. Yet newspaper articles may have greater immediacy if they use the present or future tenses where appropriate.

The perfect and pluperfect tenses also serve a purpose, often making accounts more pointed, and so more interesting. A few rough rules:

The pluperfect should be used for events that punctuate

past continuance: *He grew up in post-war Germany, where he had seen the benefits of hard work.*

If you use the past simple (aorist) tense, put a time or date to the event: *He died on April 11th.*

If you cannot, or do not want to, pin down the occasion in this way, use the perfect tense: *He has died,* or the present, *He is dead.* These imply continuance.

So does the imperfect tense: *He was a long time dying.*

See also **may and might**.

ground rules Just as *house rules* are the rules of the particular house, so *ground rules* are *the rules of the particular ground* (or grounds). They are not *basic* or *general rules.*

halve is a transitive verb, so deficits can double but not *halve*. They must *be halved* or *fall by half*.

haver means to *talk nonsense*, not *dither*, *swither* or *waver*.

headings and captions set the tone: they are more read than anything else, especially in a newspaper. Use them, therefore, to draw readers in, not to repel them. That means wit (where appropriate), not bad puns; sharpness (ditto), not familiarity (call people by their last names, not their first names); originality, not clichés.

　Writers and editors, having laboured over an article, are too often ready to yank a well-known catchphrase, or the title of a film, from the front of their mind without giving the matter any more thought. They do so, presumably, in the belief that the heading is less important than the words beneath it. If you find yourself reaching for any of the following, consider yourself eligible for ritual disembowelment:

back to the future	mind the gap
bridges (or anything else) too far	new kids on the block
	$64,000 questions
China syndromes	southern discomfort
empires striking back	thirty-somethings
French connections	windows of opportunity
F-words	where's the beef?
flavours of the month	could do better (a favourite
generation X	with education stories)
kinder	taxing times (tax stories)
gentler hearts and minds	

　On October 18th 2004 an *Economist* reader wrote as follows:

SIR – Your newspaper this week contains headlines derived from the following film titles: "As Good As It Gets", "Face-Off", "From

Russia With Love", "The Man Who Planted Trees", "Up Close and Personal" and "The Way of the Warrior". Also employed are "the Iceman Cometh", "Measure for Measure", "The Tyger" and "War and Peace" – to say nothing of the old stalwart, "Howard's Way".

Is this a competition, or do your sub-editors need to get out more?

Tom Braithwaite,
London

See also **clichés, journalese and slang.**

health care The American system of *health care* (adjective, *health-care*) for the poor is *Medicaid*, and for the elderly is *Medicare*. Canada's national health-care system is also called *Medicare*.

healthy If you think something is *desirable* or *good*, say so. Do not call it *healthy*.

heresy *see* **apostasy.**

hoards, hordes Few secreted treasures (*hoards*) are multitudes on the move (*hordes*).

Hobson's choice is not *the lesser of two evils*; it is *no choice at all.*

holistic properly refers to a theory developed by Jan Smuts, who argued that, through creative evolution, nature tended to form wholes greater than the sum of the parts.

homeland Although it is now used as a synonym for your domestic territory, your homeland is your *native land*, your *motherland* or even your *fatherland*.

homogeneous, homogenous *Homogeneous* means of the same kind or nature. *Homogenous* means similar because of common descent.

homosexual Since this word comes from the Greek word *homos* (same), not the Latin word *homo* (man), it applies as much to women as to men. It is therefore as daft to write *homosexuals and lesbians* as to write *people and women*.

hopefully By all means begin an article hopefully, but never write: *Hopefully, it will be finished by Wednesday.* Try *with luck, if all goes well, it is hoped that...*

horrible words Words that are horrible to one writer may not be horrible to another, but if you are a writer for whom no words are horrible, you would do well to take up some other activity. No words or phrases should be banned outright from appearing in print, but if you use any of the following you should be aware that they may have an emetic effect on some of your readers. *See also* **clichés.**

carer – and most caring expressions	looking to (meaning *intending to*)
chattering classes	matériel
facilitate	ongoing
famously	poster child
governance	prestigious
grow the business	proactive
guesstimate	rack up (profits, etc)
informed (as in *his love of language informed his memos*)	savvy
	segue
likely (meaning *probably*, rather than *probable*)	source (meaning *obtain*)
	stakeholder

hyphens There is no firm rule to help you decide which words are run together, hyphenated or left separate. If in doubt, consult a dictionary. Do not overdo the literary device of hyphenating words that are not usually linked: the stringing-together-of-lots-and-lots-of-words-and-ideas tendency can be tiresome.

1 Words with common or short prefixes

In general, try to avoid putting hyphens into words formed of one word and a short prefix.

asexual	neoliberal	preoccupied
biplane	neolithic	preordained
declassify	neologism	prepay
disfranchise	neonatal	realign
geopolitical	overdone	rearm
neoclassicism	overeducated	rearrange
neoconservative	precondition	reborn
but neo-cons	predate	redirect

reopen	subcontract	underpaid
reorder	subhuman	upended
repurchase	submachinegun	tetravalent
subcommittee	underdog	
subcontinent	underdone	

2 Words beginning with re-

Some words that begin with *re* are hyphenated to avoid confusion:

| *re-cast* | *re-present* (meaning *present again*) |
| *re-create* (meaning *create again*) | *re-sort* (meaning *sort again*) |

3 Unfamiliar combinations

Long words making unfamiliar combinations, especially if they would involve running several consonants together, may benefit from a hyphen, so:

cross-reference (a *cross reference* would be unpleasant)
demi-paradise
over-governed
under-secretary

Antidisestablishmentarianism would, however, lose its point if it were hyphenated.

See also 5 below (about words beginning anti, counter, half, inter, non and semi).

4 Fractions

Whether nouns or adjectives, these take hyphens:

| one-half | one-sixth |
| four-fifths | two-thirds |

But note that it is *a half, a fifth, a sixth.*

5 Words that begin with

agri	infra	post
anti	inter	pre
counter	mid	semi
extra	multi	ultra
half	non	

Rules vary here:

agri-business, agriculture
anti-aircraft, anti-fascist, anti-submarine (but antibiotic, anticlimax, antidote, antiseptic, antitrust)
counter-attack,counter-clockwise, counter-espionage, counter-intuitive (but counteract, countermand, counterpane)
extra-judicial, extraterrestrial, extraterritorial (but extraordinary)
half-baked, half-hearted, half-serious (but halfway)
infra-red
inter-agency, inter-county, inter-governmental (but intermediate, international, interpose)
mid-August, mid-week
multilingual, multiracial
non-combatant, non-existent, non-payment, non-violent (but nonaligned, nonconformist, nonplussed, nonstop)
postdate, post-war, pre-war
semi-automatic, semi-conscious, semi-detached
ultra-violet

6 Words beginning *Euro* or *euro*

These should be hyphenated, except:

Europhile	Eurosceptic	euro zone
Europhobe	euro area	

7 The word *worth*

A sum followed by the word *worth* needs a hyphen.

$25m-worth of goods

8 Some titles

attorney-general	lieutenant-colonel	under-secretary
director-general	major-general	vice-president
field-marshal	secretary-general	

but

deputy director	district attorney
deputy secretary	general secretary

9 Avoiding ambiguities

a little-used car	fine-tooth comb (most people	third-world war
a little used-car	do not comb their teeth)	third world war
cross complaint	high-school girl	
cross-complaint	high schoolgirl	

10 Aircraft

DC-10	MiG-23
Mirage F-1E	Lockheed P-3 Orion

(If in doubt, consult Jane's "All the World's Aircraft".)
Note that Airbus A340, BAe RJ70 do not have hyphens.

11 Calibres

The style for calibres is 50mm or 105mm with no hyphen, but 5.5-inch and 25-pounder.

12 Adjectives formed from two or more words

70-year-old judge
balance-of-payments difficulties
private-sector wages
public-sector borrowing requirement
right-wing groups (but the right wing of the party)
state-of-the-union message
value-added tax (VAT)

13 Adverbs

Adverbs do not need to be linked to participles or adjectives by hyphens in simple constructions:

The regiment was ill equipped for its task.
The principle is well established.
Though expensively educated, the journalist knew no grammar.

But if the adverb is one of two words together being used adjectivally, a hyphen may be needed:

The ill-equipped regiment was soon repulsed.
All well-established principles should be periodically challenged.

The hyphen is especially likely to be needed if the adverb is short and common, such as *ill, little, much* and *well.* Less common adverbs, including all those that end -ly, are less likely to need hyphens:

Never employ an expensively educated journalist.

14 Separating identical letters

book-keeping	re-emerge
coat-tails	re-entry
co-operate	trans-ship
pre-eminent	unco-operative
pre-empt	

Exceptions include:

overrate	overrun
overreach	underrate
override	withhold
overrule	

15 Some nouns formed from prepositional verbs

bail-out	lay-off	shake-out
build-up	pay-off	shake-up
buy-out	pull-out	stand-off
call-up	round-up	start-up
get-together	set-up	

But:

fallout	lockout
handout	payout
knockout	turnout

16 The quarters of the compass

mid-west(ern)	south-east(ern)
north-east(ern)	south-west(ern)
north-west(ern)	

17 Hybrid ethnics

Greek-Cypriot, Irish-American, etc, whether noun or adjective.

18 Makers and making

A general, though not iron, rule for *makers* and *making*: if the prefix is of one or two syllables, attach it without a hyphen to form a single word, but if the prefix is of three or more syllables, introduce a hyphen.

bookmaker	holiday-maker	steelmaker
candlestick-maker	lawmaker	tiramisu-maker
carmaker	marketmaker	troublemaker
chipmaker	peacemaker	antimacassar-maker
clockmaker	rule-maker	

Policymaker and *profitmaking* are one word and an exception. But: note *foreign-policy maker (ing)*.

19 Other words ending -*er* (-*ing*) that are similar to *maker* and *making*

The general rule should be to insert a hyphen:

arms-trader	gun-runner
copper-miner	home-owner
drug-dealer	hostage-taker
drug-trafficker	mill-owner
field-worker	truck-driver
front-runner	

But some prefixes, especially those of one syllable, can be used to form single words.

coalminer	metalworker	shipowner
farmworker	muckraker	steeplechaser
foxhunter	nitpicker	steelworker
gatekeeper	peacekeeper	taxpayer
householder	shipbroker	
landowner	shipbuilder	

Less common combinations are better written as two words:

currency trader	insurance broker
dog owner	crossword compiler
gun owner	tuba player

20 Quotes

Words gathered together in quotation marks to serve as adjectives do not usually need hyphens as well: *the "Live Free or Die" state*.

21 One word

airfield
airspace
airtime
bedfellow
bestseller
  (-ing)
bilingual
blackboard
blackout
blueprint
bookseller
businessman
bypass
cashflow
catchphrase
ceasefire
checklist
coastguard
codebreaker
comeback
commonsense (adj)
crossfire
cyberspace
dotcom
figleaf
fivefold
foothold
forever (adv, when
  it precedes the
  verb)
fourfold
foxhunter (-ing)
goodwill
grassroots (adj and
  noun)

groundsman
hairdresser
halfhearted
handpicked
handwriting
hardline
headache
hijack
hobnob
kowtow
lacklustre
landmine
laptop
logjam
loophole
lopsided
lukewarm
machinegun
minefield
multilingual
nationwide
nevertheless
newsweekly
nonetheless
offline
offshore
oilfield
online
onshore
peacetime
petrochemical
pickup truck
placename
rainforest
ringtone

roadblock
rustbelt
salesforce
seabed
shorthand
shortlist
shutdown
sidestep
soyabean
spillover
statewide
stockmarket
streetwalker
strongman
sunbelt
takeover
threefold
threshold
timetable
trademark
transatlantic
transpacific
twofold
videocassette
videodisc
wartime
watchdog
website
wildflower (adj,
  but noun wild
  flowers)
windfall
workforce
worldwide
worthwhile

22 Two words

ad hoc (always)
air base
air force
all right
any time
arm's length
any more
ballot box
birth rate
child care (noun)

common sense
  (noun)
dare say
drinks group
errand boy
for ever (when
  used after a verb)
girl friend
health care (noun)
joint venture

Land Rover
no one
photo opportunity
some day
some time
under way
vice versa
wild flowers (but
  adj, wildflower)

23 Two hyphenated words

aid-worker
aircraft-carrier
asylum-seekers
baby-boomer
balance-sheet
bell-ringer
come-uppance
court-martial (noun
  and verb)
cross-border
cross-dresser
cross-sell
death-squads
derring-do
drawing-board
end-game
end-year
faint-hearted
fault-line
front-line

fund-raiser (-ing)
hand-held
health-care (adj)
heir-apparent
home-made
home-page
hot-head
ice-cream
interest-group
kerb-crawler
know-how
laughing-stock
like-minded
long-standing
machine-tool
money-laundering
nation-building
nation-state
nest-egg
news-stand

number-plate
pot-hole
pressure-group
question-mark
rain-check
starting-point
sticking-point
stumbling-block
talking-shop
task-force
tear-gas
think-tank
time-bomb
turning-point
voice-mail
vote-winner
well-being
Wi-Fi
Wi-Max
working-party

24 Three words

ad hoc agreement (meeting, etc)
armoured personnel carrier
chiefs of staff
half a dozen
in as much

in so far
multiple rocket launcher
nuclear power station
third world war (if things get bad)

25 Three hyphenated words

A-turned-B (unless this leads to something unwieldy, so jobbing churchwarden turned captain of industry)

brother-in-law	commander-in-chief	prisoners-of-war
chock-a-block	no-man's-land	second-in-command

26 Numbers

Avoid *from 1947-50* (say *in 1947-50* or *from 1947 to 1950*) and *between 1961-65* (say *in 1961–65, between 1961 and 1965* or *from 1961 to 1965*). *See also* **figures**.

"If you take hyphens seriously, you will surely go mad" (Oxford University Press style manual).

hypothermia is what kills old folk in winter. If you say it is *hyperthermia*, that means they have been carried off by heat stroke.

iconoclasm Many good writers break the rules of English, and readers may occasionally forgive *The Economist* for doing so too. It is, however, possible to write well while showing respect for grammar and punctuation. An article may be improved by an original phrase or even an unusual word, but *The Economist* is not meant to be a work of literature. It is simply meant to be well written.

identical *with* not *to*.

ilk means *same*, so *of that ilk* means *of the place of the same name as the family*, not *of that kind*. Best avoided.

immolate means to *sacrifice*, not to *burn*.

important If something is *important*, say why and to whom. Use sparingly, and avoid such unexplained claims as *this important house, the most important painter of the 20th century*.

impractical, impracticable If something is *impracticable*, it *cannot be done*. If it's *impractical*, it is *not worth trying to do* it.

inchoate means *not fully developed* or *at an early stage*, not *incoherent* or *chaotic*.

including When *including* is used as a preposition, as it often is, it must be followed by a noun, pronoun or noun clause, not by a preposition. So *Iran needs more investment, including for its tired oil industry* is ungrammatical. The sentence should be rephrased, perhaps, as *Iran, including its tired oil industry, needs more investment*.

Indonesian names *see* **names**.

initially Try *at first*.

inverted commas (quotation marks) *see* **punctuation**.

investigations of not *into*.

Iranian names *see* **names**.

Islamic, Islamist *Islamic* means relating to Islam; it is a synonym of the adjective *Muslim*, but it is not used for a follower of Islam, who is always *Muslim*. But *Islamic art and architecture* is conventional usage.

> *Islamist* refers to those who see Islam as a political and social ideology as well as a religious one.

issues *The Economist* has issues – 51 a year – but if you think you have issues with *The Economist*, you probably mean you have *complaints, irritations* or *delivery problems*. If you disagree with *The Economist*, you may take issue with it. Be precise.

Italian names *see* **names**.

italics

> **foreign words and phrases** should be set in italics:

cabinet (French type)	*loya jirga*
dalits	*Mitbestimmung*
de rigueur	*pace*
jihad	*papabile*
glasnost	*perestroika*
in camera	*Schadenfreude*
intifada	*ujamaa*

> unless they are so familiar that they have become anglicised and so should be in roman. For example:

ad hoc	bourgeois
apartheid	café
a priori	coup d'état (but *coup de*
a propos	*foudre, coup de grâce*)
avant-garde	de facto, de jure
bona fide	dirigisme

elite	parvenu
en masse, en route	pogrom
grand prix	post mortem
in absentia	putsch
in situ	raison d'être
machismo	realpolitik
matériel	status quo
nom de guerre	vice versa
nouveau riche	vis-à-vis

Remember to put appropriate accents and diacritical signs on all foreign words in italics (and give initial capital letters to German nouns when in italics, but not if not). Make sure that the meaning of any foreign word you use is clear. *See also* **accents**.

For the Latin names of animals, plants, etc, *see* **spelling**.

newspapers and periodicals Only *The Economist* and *The Times* have *The* italicised. Thus the *Daily Telegraph*, the *New York Times*, the *Observer*, the *Spectator* (but *Le Monde*, *Die Welt*, *Die Zeit*). The *Yomiuri Shimbun* should be italicised, but you can also say the *Yomiuri*, or the *Yomiuri* newspaper, as *shimbun* simply means newspaper in Japanese. The *Nikkei* is an abbreviation (for *Nihon Keizai*) and so should not be written as *Nikkei Shimbun* as that is not strictly this financial daily's name.

books, pamphlets, plays, operas, ballets, radio and television programmes Titles are roman, not italic, with capital letters for each main word, in quotation marks. Thus: "Pride and Prejudice", "Much Ado about Nothing", "Any Questions", "Crossfire", etc. But the Bible and its books (Genesis, Ecclesiastes, John, etc), as well as the Koran, are written without inverted commas. These rules apply to footnotes as well as bodymatter.

Note that book publishers generally use italics for the titles of books, pamphlets, plays, operas, ballets, radio and television programmes.

lawsuits

Brown v Board of Education
Coatsworth v Johnson
Jarndyce v Jarndyce

If abbreviated, *versus* should always be shortened to v, with no point after it. The v should not be italic if it is not a lawsuit.

names of ships, aircraft, spacecraft

HMS Illustrious
Spirit of St Louis
Challenger

j

Japanese names *see* **names.**

jargon Avoid it. You may have to think harder if you are not to use
jargon, but you can still be precise. Technical terms should be
used in their proper context; do not use them out of it. In many
instances simple words can do the job of *exponential* (try *fast*),
interface (*frontier* or *border*) and so on. If you find yourself tempted
to write about *affirmative action* or *corporate governance*, you will
have to explain what it is; with luck, you will then not have to use
the actual expression.

Avoid, above all, the kind of jargon that tries to dignify
nonsense with seriousness:

> *The appointee ... should have a proven track record of operating at
> a senior level within a multi-site international business, preferably
> within a service- or brand-oriented environment*

declared an advertisement for a financial controller for The
Economist Group.

> *At a national level, the department engaged stakeholders positively ...
> This helped ... to improve stakeholder buy-in to agreed changes*

avowed a British civil servant in a report.

> *The City Safe T3 Resilience Project is a cross-sector initiative
> bringing together experts ... to enable multi-tier practitioner-oriented
> collaboration on resilience and counter-terrorism challenges and
> opportunities*

explained Chatham House.

Or to obscure the truth:

> *These grants will incentivise administrators and educators to apply
> relevant metrics to assess achievement in the competencies they seek to
> develop*

said a memo cited by Tony Proscio in "Bad Words for Good" (The

Edna McConnell Clark Foundation). What it meant, as Mr Proscio points out, was that the grants would be used to pay teachers who agreed to test their students.

Or simply to obfuscate:

A multi-agency project catering for holistic diversionary provision to young people for positive action linked to the community safety strategy and the pupil referral unit

was how Luton Education Authority described go-karting lessons.

Someone with good *interpersonal skills* probably just *gets on well with others*. Someone with poor *parenting skills* is probably a *bad father* or a *bad mother*. *Negative health outcomes* are probably *illness* or *death*. *Intelligent media brands for the high-end audience that clients value* are presumably *good publications for rich people*.

See also **due process**.

jib, gibe, gybe

jib (noun)	*sail* or *boom of a crane*
jib (verb)	to *balk* or *shy*
gibe (verb)	to *scoff* or *flout*
gibe (noun)	*taunt*
gybe (verb)	to *alter course*

Don't *jibe*.

journalese and slang Do not be too free with slang like *He really hit the big time in 1994*. Slang, like metaphors, should be used only occasionally if it is to have effect. Avoid expressions used only by journalists, such as giving people *the thumbs up*, *the thumbs down* or *the green light*. Stay clear of *gravy trains* and *salami tactics*. Do not use *the likes of*, or *Big Pharma* (*big drug firms*).

And avoid words and expressions that are ugly or overused, such as:

the bottom line
crisis
guesstimate (use *guess*)
key
major (unless something else nearby is minor)
massive (as in massive inflation)

meaningful
perceptions
prestigious
schizophrenic (unless the context is medical)
significant

Politicians are often said to be highly *visible* or *high-profile*, when *conspicuous* or *prominent* would be more appropriate. Regulations are sometimes said to be designed to create *transparency*, which presumably means *openness*. *Governance* usually means *government*, but not when used with *corporate*. Elections described as *too close to call* are usually just *close*. *Ethics violations*, if they are not crimes, are likely to be *shenanigans*, *scandalous behaviour* or mere *misdemeanours*.

Try not to be predictable, especially predictably jocular. Spare your readers any mention of *mandarins* when writing about the civil service, of *their lordships* when discussing the House of Lords, and of *comrades* when analysing communist parties. Must all stories about Central Asia include a reference to the *Great Game*? Must all lawns be *manicured*? Must all small towns in the old confederacy be called the *buckle on the Bible belt*? Are drug-traffickers inevitably *barons*? Must starlets and models always be *scantily clad*? Is there any other kind of *wonk* than a *policy wonk*?

Resist saying *This will be no panacea*. When you find something that is indeed a *panacea* (or a *magic* or *silver bullet*), that will indeed be news. Similarly, hold back from offering the reassurance *There is no need to panic*. Instead, ask yourself exactly when there is a need to panic.

In general, try to make your writing fresh. It will seem stale if it reads like hackneyed journalese. One weakness of journalists, who on daily newspapers may plead that they have little time to search for the apposite word, is a love of the ready-made, seventh-hand phrase. Lazy journalists are always at home in *oil-rich* country A, ruled by *ailing* President B, the *long-serving strongman*, who is, according to the *chattering classes*, not *squeaky clean* but a *wily political operator* – hence the present *uneasy peace* – but, after his recent *watershed* (or *ground-breaking* or *landmark* or *sea-change*) decision to arrest his prime minister (the *honeymoon is over*), will soon face a *bloody uprising* in the *breakaway* south. Similarly, lazy business journalists always enjoy describing the problems of *troubled* company C, a victim of the *revolution* in the gimbal-pin industry (change is always revolutionary in such industries), which, *well-placed insiders* predict, will be riven by a *make-or-break* strike unless one of the *major players* makes an 11th-hour (or *last-ditch*) intervention in a *marathon* negotiating session.

Prose such as this is often freighted with codewords (writers apply *respected* to someone they approve of, *militant* to someone they disapprove of, *prestigious* to something you won't have heard of). The story usually starts with *First the good news*, inevitably to be followed in due course by *Now the bad news*. An alternative is *Another week, another bomb* (giving rise to thoughts of *Another story, another hackneyed opening*). Or, *It was the best of times, it was the worst of times* – and certainly the feeblest of introductions. A quote will then be inserted, attributed to *one* (never *an*) *industry analyst*, and often the words *If, and it's a big if* ... Towards the end, after an admission that the author has no idea what is going on, there is always room for *One thing is certain*, before rounding off the article with *As one wag put it* ...

See also **clichés**, **headings and captions**, **metaphors**.

key A *key* may be *major* or *minor*, but not *low*. Few of the decisions, people, industries described as *key* are truly *indispensable*, and fewer still *open locks*.

This overused word is a noun and, like many nouns, may be used adjectivally (as in the *key ministries*). Do not, however, use it as a free-standing adjective, as in *The choice of running-mate is key*.

Do not use *key* to make the subject of your sentence more important than he, she or it really is. The words *key players* are a sure sign of a puffed-up story and a lazy mind.

Korean names *see* **names.**

Kyrgyzstan, Kirgiz *see* **countries and their inhabitants.**

L

lag If you *lag* transitively, you lag a pipe or a loft. Anything failing to keep up with a front-runner, rate of growth, fourth-quarter profit or whatever is *lagging behind it*.

last The *last* issue of *The Economist* implies its extinction; prefer *last week's* or the *latest* issue. *Last year*, in 2006, means 2005; if you mean the 12 months up to the time of writing, write the *past year*. The same goes for the *past* month, *past* week, *past* (not *last*) ten years. *Last week* is best avoided; anyone reading it several days after publication may be confused. *This week* is permissible.

Latin names When it is necessary to use a Latin name for animals, plants, etc, follow the standard practice. Thus for all creatures higher than viruses, write the binomial name in italics, giving an initial capital to the first word (the genus): *Turdus turdus*, the songthrush; *Metasequoia glyptostroboides*, the dawn redwood; *Culicoides clintoni*, a species of midge. This rule also applies to *Homo sapiens* and to such uses as *Homo economicus*. On second mention, the genus may be abbreviated (*T. turdus*). In some species, such as dinosaurs, the genus alone is used in lieu of a common name: *Diplodocus*, *Tyrannosaurus*. Also *Drosophila*, a fruitfly favoured by geneticists. But *Escherichia coli*, a bacterium also favoured by geneticists, is known universally as *E. coli*, even on first mention.

leverage If you really cannot find a way of avoiding the word *leverage*, you must explain what it means (unless it is simply *the use of a lever to gain a mechanical advantage*). In its technical sense, as a noun, it may mean *the ratio of long-term debt to total capital employed*. But note that *operating leverage* and *financial leverage* are different. The verb is even viler than the noun (try *lever*). *See also* **gearing**.

liberal in Europe, someone who believes above all in the freedom of the individual; in the United States, someone who believes in the progressive tradition of Franklin D. Roosevelt. Such is the confusion that an article on America's Supreme Court in *The Economist* of July 2nd 2005 had Anthony Kennedy as a *conservative* (meaning favourable to displays of the Ten Commandments on government property) on one page and a *liberal* (meaning favourable to big government and big business) on the next. The following week *liberal* was used in an article on Germany to mean favourable to labour-market reform, indirect taxation and cuts in subsidies.

lifestyle Prefer *way of life.*

like governs nouns and pronouns, not verbs and clauses. So *as in America* not *like in America, as I was saying,* not *like I was saying, as Grandma used to make them,* not *like Grandma used to make them,* etc. English has no "unas" equivalent to *unlike,* so you must rephrase the sentence if you are tempted to write *unlike in this context, unlike at Christmas,* or *unlike when I was a child.*

   If you find yourself writing *She looked like she had had enough* or *It seemed like he was running out of puff,* you should replace *like* with *as if* or *as though,* and you probably need the subjunctive: *She looked as if she had had enough, It seemed as if he were running out of puff.*

"*Like the hart panteth for the water brooks I pant for a revival of Shakespeare's 'Like You Like It'.*
I can see tense draftees relax and purr
When the sergeant barks, 'Like you were.'
– And don't try to tell me that our well has been defiled by immigration;
Like goes Madison Avenue, like so goes the nation."
(Ogden Nash)

   But *authorities like Fowler and Gowers* is a perfectly acceptable alternative to *authorities such as Fowler and Gowers.*

likely Avoid such constructions as *He will likely announce the date on Monday* and *The price will likely fall when results are posted Friday.* Prefer *He is likely to announce ...* or *It is likely that the price will ...*

locate (in all its forms) can usually be replaced by something less ugly. *The missing scientist was located* means he was *found. The diplomats will meet at a secret location* means either that they will meet *in a* secret *place* or that they will meet *secretly*. A *company* located in *Texas* is simply *a company in Texas*.

lower case *see* **capitals**.

luxurious, luxuriant *Luxurious* means *indulgently pleasurable*; *luxuriant* means *exuberant* or *profuse*. A tramp may have a *luxuriant beard* but not a *luxurious life*.

masterful, masterly *Masterful* means *imperious*; *masterly* means *skilled*.

may and might are not always interchangeable, and you may want *may* more often than you think. If in doubt, try *may* first. *I might be wrong, but I think it will rain later* should be *I may be wrong, but I think it will rain later.*

Much of the trouble arises from the fact that *may* becomes *might* in both the subjunctive and in some constructions using past tenses. *Mr Blair admits that weapons of mass destruction may never be found* becomes, in the past, *Mr Blair admitted that weapons of mass destruction might never be found.*

Conditional sentences using the subjunctive also need *might.* Thus *If Mr Bush were to win the election, he might make his horse ambassador to the UN.* This could be rephrased by *If Mr Bush wins the election, he may make his horse ambassador to the UN.* Conditional sentences stating something contrary to fact, however, need *might: If pigs had wings, birds might raise their eyebrows.*

The facts are crucial. *New research shows Tutankhamun may have died of a broken leg* is fine, if indeed that is what the research shows. *New research shows Tutankhamun might have died of a broken leg* is not fine, unless it is followed by something like *if his mummy hadn't dressed the wound before it became infected.* This, though, is saying something quite different. In the first example, it is clear both that Tutankhamun died and that a broken leg may have been responsible. In the second, it is clear only that his wound was dressed; as a result, Tutankhamun seems to have survived.

Similarly, *John Kerry might make French lessons mandatory for Republicans* is fine before the election (when it is unclear whether he will win). After the election (when he has lost), *John Kerry may make French lessons mandatory for Republicans* becomes absurd, though *John Kerry may start learning German* does not. *John Kerry might have made French lessons mandatory for Republicans* is, however, fine.

Sometimes it is all right to use *might* if part of the sentence is understood though not explicitly stated: *Tony Blair would never tell a fib, but Jeffrey Archer might (if circumstances demanded or if he had forgotten the truth). That might be actionable (if a judge said it was).*

Facts remain crucial: *I might have called him a liar (but I didn't have the guts). I may have called him a liar (I can't now remember).*

Do not write *George Bush might believe in education, but he calls the Greeks Grecians.* It should be *George Bush may believe in education, but he calls the Greeks Grecians.* Only if you are putting forward a hypothesis that may or may not be true are *may* and *might* interchangeable. Thus *If George Bush studies hard, he may (or might) learn the difference between Greek and Grecian.*

Could is sometimes useful as an alternative to *may* and *might*: *His coalition could (or may) collapse.* But take care. Does *He could call an election in May* mean *He may call an election in May* or *He would be allowed to call an election in May*?

Do not use *may* or *might* when the appropriate verb is *to be*. *His colleagues wonder how far the prime minister may go. The danger for them is that they may all lose their seats* should be *His colleagues wonder how far the prime minister will go. The danger for them is that they will all lose their seats.*

See also **grammar and syntax**.

measures *see* Part 3.

media Prefer *press and television* or, if the context allows it, just *press*. If you have to use the *media*, remember they are plural.

metaphors "A newly invented metaphor assists thought by evoking a visual image," said Orwell, "while on the other hand a metaphor which is technically 'dead' (eg, iron resolution) has in effect reverted to being an ordinary word and can generally be used without loss of vividness. But in between these two classes there is a huge dump of worn-out metaphors which are merely used because they save people the trouble of inventing phrases for themselves."

Every issue of *The Economist* contains scores of metaphors:

gay soldiers booted back on to Civvy Street, asset-price bubbles pricked, house prices getting monetary medicine, gauntlets thrown down, ideas floated, tides turned, accounts embraced, barrages of criticism unleashed, retailing behemoths arriving with a splash, foundering chains, both floods and flocks of job-seekers, limelight hogged, inflation ignited, the ratio of chiefs to Indians, landmark patent challenges, drugs giants taking steps towards the dark side, cash-strapped Fiat, football clubs teetering on the brink, prices inching up (or peaking, spiking or even going north), a leaden overhang of shares, giddying rises, rosy scenarios being painted, a fat lady not singing

Some of these are tired, and will therefore tire the reader. Most are so exhausted that they may be considered dead, and are therefore permissible. But use all metaphors, dead or alive, sparingly, otherwise you will make trouble for yourself.

An issue of *The Economist* chosen at random had:

a package cutting the budget deficit, the administration loth to sign on to higher targets, the lure of eastern Germany as a springboard to the struggling markets of eastern Europe, west Europeanness helping to dilute an image, someone finding a pretext to stall the process before looking for a few integrationist crumbs, a spring clean that became in the next sentence a stalking-horse for greater spending, and Michelin axing jobs in painful surgery

Within four consecutive sentences in another issue lay:

a chance to lance the Israel-Palestine boil, Americans and Europeans sitting on their hands while waiting for Israel to freeze settlement building, or for Palestinians to corral militants, the need to stop the two sides playing the "after you" game, a confidence-building and money-begging conference followed by a shot in the arm for the Americans

Another article included this:

"During a long and improbable life Spiegel sloughed off more skins than a bed of snakes, and a biographer's first task is to keep their footing."

An attempt to *"defuse simmering tensions"* was taken out of another article before it was published, but this slipped through:

"Like Japan's before it, America's stockmarket bubble was inflated on the back of a mountain of corporate debt. So onerous was this debt that many American companies were forced to the wall."

mete You may *mete out* punishment, but if it is to fit the crime it is *meet*.

metrics are the *theory of measurement*. Do not use the term as a pretentious word for *figures*, *dimensions* or *measurements* themselves, as in "*I can't take the metrics I'm privileged to and work my way to a number in [that] range*" (General George Metz, talking about the number of insurgents killed in Iraq).

migrate is intransitive. Do not *migrate people* or *things*.

millionaire The time has gone when young women would think that the term *millionaire* adequately described the man who broke the bank at Monte Carlo. If you wish to use it, make it plain that *millionaire* refers to income (in dollars or pounds), not to capital. Otherwise try *plutocrat* or *rich man*.

mitigate, militate *Mitigate* mollifies; *militate* does the opposite.

monopoly, monopsony A *monopolist* is the sole seller. A sole buyer is a *monopsonist*. *See* **oligopoly**.

moot in British English means *arguable*, *doubtful* or *open to debate*. Americans often use it to mean *hypothetical* or *academic*, ie *of no practical significance*. Prefer the British usage.

mortar If not a *vessel* in which herbs, etc are pounded with a pestle, a *mortar* is a *piece of artillery* for throwing a shell, bomb or lifeline. Do not write *He was hit by a mortar* unless you mean he was struck by the artillery piece itself, which is improbable.

move Do not use *move* (noun) if you mean *decision*, *bid*, *deal* or something more precise. But *move* (verb) rather than *relocate*.

names

For guidance on spelling people's names, see below. As with all names, spell them the way the person concerned has requested, if a preference has been expressed. Here are some names that cause spelling difficulties.

Issaias Afwerki (Mr Issaias)
Gianni Agnelli
Muhammad Farrah Aideed
Askar Akayev
Heidar Aliyev
Joaquín Almunia
Yasser Arafat
Bashar Assad
José María Aznar
José Manuel Barroso (no need to include his third name, Durão)
Traian Basescu
Deniz Baykal
Zine el-Abidine Ben Ali
Chadli Benjedid
Ritt Bjerregaard
Frits Bolkestein
Mangosuthu Buthelezi
Cuauhtémoc Cardenas
Josep Lluis Carod-Rivera
Jean-Pierre Chevènement
Emilio Chuayffet
Wlodzimierz Cimoszewicz
Uncle Tom Cobbleigh
José Cutileiro
Poul Dalsager
Carlo De Benedetti

Gaston Defferre
Gianni De Michelis
Ciriaco De Mita
Yves-Thibault de Silguy
Carlo Ripa di Meana
Fyodor Dostoyevsky
Jokhar Dudayev
Mikulas Dzurinda
Recep Tayyip Erdogan
King Fahd
Joschka Fischer
Boris Fyodorov
Gandhi
Hans-Dietrich Genscher
Valéry Giscard d'Estaing (Mr Giscard d'Estaing)
Felipe González
Mikhail Gorbachev
Habsburgs
Gulbuddin Hikmatyar
Elias Hrawi
Saddam Hussein
Juan José Ibarretxe
Jaba Iosseliani
Alija Izetbegovic
Radovan Karadzic
Mikhail Khodorkovsky
Nikita Khrushchev

Vojislav Kostunica
Aleksander Kwasniewski
Kim Dae-jung
Kim Jong Il
Costas Karamanlis
Bob Kerrey (Nebraska)
John Kerry (Massachusetts)
Sergei Kozalev
Alain Lamassoure
Alyaksandr Lukashenka
Milan Martic
Ahmad Shah Masoud
Slobodan Milosevic
Ratko Mladic
Mahathir Mohamad
King Mohammed of Morocco
Milan Mrsic
Hosni Mubarak
Muhammad the Prophet
Franz Müntefering
Nursultan Nazarbayev
Binyamin Netanyahu
Saparmurat Niyazov
Gaafar Numeiri
Andrej Olechowski
Mullah Mohammed Omar
Karl Otto Pöhl
Velupillai Prabhakaran
Viktor Pynzenyk
Muammar Qaddafi
Burhanuddin Rabbani
Yitzhak Rabin
Ali Akbar Rafsanjani
Cyril Ramaphosa
Prince Ranariddh
Rodrigo de Rato (Mr de Rato)

Condoleezza Rice
Nikolai Ryzhkov
Mikhail Saakashvili
Andrei Sakharov
Ali Abdullah Saleh
Nicolas Sarkozy
Wolfgang Schäuble
Gerhard Schröder
Arnold Schwarzenegger
Mohammed Zahir Shah
Yitzhak Shamir
Eduard Shevardnadze
Haris Silajdic
Banharn Silpa-archa
José Sócrates
Javier Solana
Alexander Solzhenitsyn
Franz Josef Strauss
Adolfo Suárez (Spain)
Aung San Suu Kyi (Miss Suu Kyi)
Jean Tiberi
Yulia Tymoshenko
Hans van den Broek (Mr Van den Broek)
Karel Van Miert (Mr Van Miert)
Atal Bihari Vajpayee
Tabaré Vázquez (Dr)
Hans-Jochen Vogel
Grigory Yavlinsky
Victor Yushchenko
José Luis Rodríguez Zapatero
Vladimir Zhirinovsky
Goodwill Zwelithini
Gennady Zyuganov

Afghan

Gulbuddin Hikmatyar
Ahmad Shah Masoud
Mullah Mohammed Omar

Burhanuddin Rabbani
Mazar-i-Sharif

Arabic names and words

Al, al- Try to leave out the *Al*, *Al-*, *al* or *al-*. This is common
practice with well-known figures like Bashar Assad (not
al-Assad) and Muammar Qaddafi (not al-Qaddafi). Many
names, however, would look peculiar without *al-*, so with
less well-known people it should be included (lower case,
usually followed by a hyphen). On subsequent mentions,
it can be dropped. *Bin* (son of) must be repeated: *Osama
bin Laden*, thereafter *Mr bin Laden*. But it is often ignored
in alphabetisation.

The *Al-*, *Al-*, *al* or *al-* (or *Ad-*, *Ar-*, *As-*, etc) before most
Arab towns can be dropped (so *Baquba* not *al-Baquba*,
Ramadi not *ar-Ramadi*). But *al-Quds*, since it is the Arab
name for Jerusalem, will be important in any context in
which it appears.

Abdullah, Prince
Habib Achour
Sabah al-Ahmad, Sheikh
Ain Saheb
Abu Alaa (aka Ahmad Qurei)
Bourj al-Barajneh
Iyad Allawi
al-Qaeda
Abu Ammar
Aqaba
Yasser Arafat
Arslan
Bashar Assad
Hafez Assad
Rifaat Assad
Awali River
Tariq Aziz
Baalbek
Baath
Badawi
Bahrain
Baquba
Mohamed El Baradei
Marwan Barghouti
Mustafa Barghouti

Masoud Barzani
Omar Bashir
Tahsin Bashir
Basra
Zine el-Abidine Ben Ali
Nabih Berri
Bhamdoun
Borujerd
Habib Bourguiba
Wassila Bourguiba
Boutros Boutros-Ghali
Bubiyan
Ahmed Chalabi
Ahmed Ben Chadli
Camille Chamoun
Chouf (the)
Dahlan
Dawah
Dezful
Dhahran
Dhofar
Raymond Edde
Khaled Fahoum
Hisham Fakhri
Falluja

Fatah
Suleiman Franjieh
Elias Freij
Gaza Strip (and City)
Amin Gemayel
Pierre Gemayel
Driss Guiga
George Habash
Hadith
haj
Hamma
Rafik Hariri
Hanni Hassan
Khalid Hassan
Hassan, Crown Prince
Nayef Hawatmeh
Hizbullah
Homs
hudna
Hussein, Saddam
Hussein, King
Ibn Khaldoun
Ahmad Jibril
intifada
Islamic Jihad
Abu Iyyad
Ibrahim al-Jaafari (Dr)
Jalloud
jamaat islamiya
Jeddah
jihad
Abu Jihad
Jubail
Kamal Jumblatt
Walid Jumblatt
Jumhuri Islami
Rashid Karami
Karbala
Abdel Halim Khaddam
Karim Khalaf
Khamenei
Iqlim al-Kharroub

Kirkuk
Klaiat
Antoine Lahd
Emile Lahoud
Larak
Latakia
Layoun (aka Al-Ayoun)
Abu Lutf
Adel Abd al-Mahdi
Sadiq el Mahdi
Majnoon
Marakeh
Maronite
Masirah island
Masri Taher
Abu Mazen (aka Mahmoud
   Abbas)
Mosul
Moukhtara
Rene Muawad
Hosni Mubarak
Muhammad the Prophet
mujahideen (singular,
   mujahid)
Mukhabarat
Murabitoun
Muslim
Nabatiya
Najaf
Naqoura
Nasiriya
Abu Nidal
Jaafar Numeiri
Ahmad Obeidat
Adnan Abu Odeh
Hannah Odeh
Pakredoumi
Penjwin
Qaboos, Sultan
Muammar Qaddafi
Farouq Qaddoumi
Qadisiyyah

Fahd Qawasmeh
Ahmed Qurei
Qurnah
Massoud Rajavi
Ramadi
Ras Tanura
Riyadh
Anwar Sadat
Muqtada al-Sadr
Abu Saleh
Ali Abdullah Saleh
Elie Salem
Saeb Salem
Kemal Salibi
Samarra
Saud al-Faisal, Prince
Shabaan
Abu Shakra
Mehdi Shamseddin, Sheikh
Laila Sharaf
Sharjah
Sharm el-Sheikh
Shatt al-Arab
Rashad Shawa

sheikh
Shuqairi
Ali al-Sistani (Grand
  Ayatollah)
Souq al-Gharb
Strait of Hormuz
Masjid Sulayman
Tal Afar
Jalal Talabani
Tawheed
Mustafa Tlas
Tulkarm
Tumbs
Umm al Aish
Shafiq Wazzan
Ahmed Zaki Yamani, Sheikh
Ghazi al-Yawar
Yanbu
Yarmuk
Taha Yasin Ramadan
Ghassem Ali Zahir-Nejad
Abu Musab al-Zarqawi
Zayed, Sheikh
Riyad Abu Zied

See also **Arabic**, page 18.

Bangladeshi If the name includes the Islamic definite article, it should be lower-case and without any hyphens: *Mujib ur Rahman*.

Belarusian If *Belarusians* (not *Belarussians*) wish to be known by the Belarusian form of their names (*Ihor*, *Vital* and *Life-President Alyaksandr Lukashenka*), so be it.

Cambodian On second reference, repeat both names: *Mr Hun Sen, Mr Sam Rainsy*.

Central Asian For those with Russified names, *see* **Russian**.

Askar Akayev
Heidar Aliyev

Nursultan Nazarbayev
Saparmurat Niyazov

Chinese In general, follow the pinyin spelling of Chinese names, which has replaced the old Wade-Giles system, except for historical references, and people and places outside mainland China. *Peking* is therefore *Beijing* and *Mao* is *Zedong*, not *Tse-tung*.

There are no hyphens in pinyin spelling. So:

Deng Xiaoping	Mao Zedong (Tse-tung)
Guangdong (Kwangtung)	Qingdao (Tsingtao)
Guangzhou (Canton)	Tianjin (Tientsin)
Hu Yaobang	Xinjiang (Sinkiang)
Jiang Qing (Mrs Mao)	Zhao Ziyang

But

Chiang Kai-shek	Li Ka-shing
Hong Kong	Lee Teng-hui

The family name comes first, so *Deng Xiaoping* becomes *Mr Deng* on a later mention.

Note that *Peking University* and *Tsinghua University* have kept their pre-pinyin romanised names.

Dutch If using first name and surname together, *vans* and *dens* are lower case: *Dries van Agt* and *Joop den Uyl*. But without their first names they become *Mr Van Agt* and *Mr Den Uyl*; *Hans van den Broek* becomes *Mr Van den Broek*. These rules do not always apply to Dutch names in Belgium and South Africa; *Karel Van Miert*, for instance (as well as *Mr Van Miert*).

Note that *Flemings* speak *Dutch*.

French Any *de* is likely to be lower case, unless it starts a sentence. *De Gaulle* goes up; *Charles de Gaulle* and plain *de Gaulle* go down. So does *Yves-Thibault de Silguy*.

German Any *von* is likely to be upper case only at the start of a sentence.

Indonesian Generally straightforward, but:

Abu Bakar Basyir	Muhammadiyah	Syafii Maarif
Jemaah Islamiah	Nahdlatul Ulama	

Some Indonesians have only one name. On first mention give it to them unadorned: *Budiono*. Thereafter add the appropriate title: *Mr Budiono*. For those who have several names, be sure to get rid of the correct ones on second and subsequent mentions: *Susilo Bambang Yudhoyono*, for example, becomes *President* (or *Mr*) *Yudhoyono*.

Iranian *Farsi*, an Arabised version of *Parsi* (meaning *of Persia*), is the term Iranians use for their language. In English, the language is properly called *Persian*.

The language spoken in Iran (and Tajikistan) is *Persian*, not *Farsi*.

Here is a list of some proper names and words.

Abadan	Khuzestan
Bandar Abbas	Nureddin Kianouri
Mahmoud Ahmadinejad	Lavan island
Ahwaz	Mahdavi-Kani, Ayatollah
Ali-Reza Amini, Ayatollah	*maqnaeh*
Bahai	Hossein-Ali Montazeri,
Abolhassan Bani-Sadr	Ayatollah
baseej	Hossein Moussavi
Mehdi Bazargan	Abu Musa
Ali Akbar Belayati	Abdollah Nouri
Bushehr	Pahlavi, Mohammad Reza,
Golpayegani, Ayatollah	Shah
Mehdi Hashemi	Qeshm
Hizbullah	Ali Akbar Rafsanjani
Hojjatieh	Rezaiyeh
Kermanshah	Yusef Saanei, Ayatollah
Keyhan	Shatt al-Arab
Ali Khamenei, Ayatollah	Abdokarim Soroush
Kharg island	Strait of Hormuz
Muhammad Khatami	Jalaluddin Taheri, Ayatollah
Mohammad Khoeinia,	Taqi Banki
Ayatollah	Tehran
Ahmad Khomeini	Tudeh
Ruhollah Khomeini,	Tumbs
Ayatollah	*velayat-e faqih*
Bandar Khomeini	Yahyaoui
Khorramshahr	

Italian Any *De* is likely to be upper case, but there are exceptions (especially among aristocrats such as *Carlo Ripa di Meana*), so check.

Japanese Although the Japanese put the family name first in their own language (*Koizumi Junichiro*), they generally reverse the order in western contexts. So:

Junichiro Koizumi Heizo Takenaka Shintaro Ishihara etc.

Korean South Koreans have changed their convention to *Kim Dae-jung*. But North Koreans, at least pending unification, have stuck to *Kim Jong Il*. Kim is the family name.

The South Korean party formed in 2003 is the Uri Party.

Pakistani If the name includes the Islamic definite article *ul*, it should be lower case and without any hyphens: *Zia ul Haq, Mahbub ul Haq* (but *Sadruddin, Mohieddin* and *Saladin* are single words).

The genitive *e* is hyphenated: *Jamaat-e-Islami, Muttahida Majlis-e-Amal*.

Russian Each approach to transliterating Russian has drawbacks. The following rules aim for phonetic accuracy, except when that conflicts with widely accepted usage.

No *y* before *e* after consonants: *Belarus, perestroika, Oleg, Lev, Medvedev*. (The actual pronunciation is somewhere between *e* and *ye*.)

1   Where pronunciation dictates, put a *y* before the *a* or *e* at the start of a word or after a vowel:

Aliyev not Aliev	Dudayev
Baluyevsky	Yavlinsky
Dostoyevsky	Yevgeny not Evgeny

2   Words spelled with *e* in Russian but pronounced *yo* should be spelled *yo*. Thus:

Fyodorov not Fedorov
Seleznyov not Seleznev
Pyotr not Petr

But stick to *Gorbachev, Khrushchev* and other famous ones that would otherwise look odd.

3   With words that could end *-i, -ii, -y* or *-iy*, use *-y* after consonants and *-i* after vowels. This respects both phonetics and common usage.

Georgy   Yury
Gennady   Zhirinovsky
Nizhny

But:

Bolshoi   Rutskoi
Nikolai   Sergei

Exception (because conventional): *Tolstoy*.

4   Replace *dzh* with j.

Jokhar, Jugashvili (for Stalin; bowing to convention, give his first name as *Josef*, not *Iosif*).

5   Prefer *Aleksandr, Viktor, Eduard, Pyotr* to *Alexander, Victor, Edward, Peter*, unless the person involved has clearly chosen an anglicised version. But keep the familiar spelling for historical figures such as *Alexander Nevsky, Alexander Solzhenitsyn* and *Peter the Great*.

Singaporean names have no hyphens and the family name comes first: *Lee Kuan Yew* (thereafter *Mr Lee*).

Spanish Spaniards sometimes have several names, including two surnames. On first mention, spell out in full all the names of such people, if they use both surnames. Thereafter the normal practice is to write the first surname only, so *Joaquín Almunia Amann* becomes *Mr Almunia* on second and subsequent mentions.

Often, though, the second surname is used only by people whose first surname is common, such as *Fernández, López* or *Rodríguez*. To avert confusion with others, they may choose to keep both their surnames when they are referred to as Mr This or Mr That, so *Miguel Ángel Fernández Ordóñez*, for instance, becomes *Mr Fernández Ordóñez*, just as *Andrés Manuel López Obrador* becomes *Mr López Obrador* and *Juan Fernando López Aguilar* becomes *Mr López Aguilar*. A few people, notably *José Luis Rodríguez Zapatero*, choose to have their names shortened to just the second of their surnames, so he becomes *Mr Zapatero*.

Although on marriage Spanish women sometimes informally add their husband's name (after a *de*) to their own, they do not usually change their legal name, merely adopting *Señora* in place of *Señorita*. Unless the woman you are writing about prefers some other title, you should likewise simply change from *Miss* to *Mrs*.

Swiss personal names follow the rules for the two languages mostly spoken in Switzerland: French and German.

Turk, Turkic, Turkmen, Turkoman, etc *see* **Countries and their inhabitants.**

Ukrainian After an orgy of retransliteration from their Russian versions, a convention has emerged. Its main rules are these.

1 Since Ukrainian has no g, use *h*:

Hryhory Heorhy Ihor (not *Grigory, Georgy, Igor*)

Exception: *Georgy Gongadze.*

2 Render the Ukrainian i as an i, and the И as a y. So *Vital, Kharkiv, Chernivtsi*; but *Volodymyr, Yanukovych, Tymoshenko, Borys, Zhytomyr.* Change words ending -iy to -y (*Hryhory*).

However, respect the wishes of those Ukrainians who wish to be known by their Russian names, or by an anglicised transliteration of them: *Alexander Morozov.*

Vietnamese names have no hyphens and the family name comes first:

Ho Chi Minh
Tran Duc Luong (thereafter Mr Tran)

neither ... nor *see* **none.**

new words and new uses for old words Part of the strength and vitality of English is its readiness to welcome new words and expressions, and to accept new meanings for old words. Yet such meanings and uses often depart as quickly as they arrived, and the early adopter risks looking like a super-trendy if he brings them into service too soon. Moreover, to anyone of sensibility some new words are more welcome than others, even if no two people of sensibility would agree on which words should be ushered in and which kept firmly on the doorstep.

Before grabbing the latest usage, ask yourself a few questions. Is it likely to pass the test of time? If not, are you using it to show just how cool you are? Has it already become a cliché? Does it do a job no other word or expression does just as well? Does it rob

the language of a useful or well-liked meaning? Is it being adopted
to make the writer's prose sharper, crisper, more euphonious,
easier to understand – in other words, better? Or to make it seem
more with it (yes, that was cool once, just as cool is cool now),
more pompous, more bureaucratic or more politically correct – in
other words, worse? *See also* **clichés**, **horrible words**, **jargon**,
journalese and slang.

none usually takes a singular verb. So does *neither* (or *either*) *A nor*
(*or*) *B*, unless B is plural, as in *Neither the Dutchman nor the Danes*
have done it, where the verb agrees with the element closest to it.
Similarly,

"*Come live with me and be my love,*
And we will all the pleasures prove
That hills and valleys, dales and fields,
Or woods or steepy mountain yields."
(Christopher Marlowe)

nor means *and not*, so should not be preceded by *and*.

O

oblivious If you are *oblivious* of something, you are not simply *unaware* of it. You have *forgotten* it or are *absent-mindedly unaware* of it.

offensive In Britain, *offensive* (as an adjective) means *rude*; in America, it often means *attacking*. Similarly, to the British an *offence* is usually a *crime* or *transgression*; to Americans it is often an *offensive*, or the counterpart to a *defence*.

oligopoly Limited competition between a small number of producers or sellers. *See also* **monopoly**, **monopsony**.

only Put *only* as close as you can to the words it qualifies. Thus *These animals mate only in June.* To say *They only mate in June* implies that in June they do nothing else.

one Try to avoid *one* as a personal pronoun. *You* will often do instead.

onto *On* and *to* should be run together when they are closely linked as in *He pranced onto the stage.* If, however, the sense of the sentence makes the *on* closer to the preceding word, or the *to* closer to the succeeding word, than they are to each other, keep them separate: *He pranced on to the next town* or *He pranced on to wild applause.*

overwhelm means *submerge utterly, crush, bring to sudden ruin.* Majority votes, for example, seldom do any of these things. As for the ethnic Albanians in Kosovo, although 90% of the population, they turned out to be an *overwhelmed majority*, not an *overwhelming one*, until NATO stepped in.

oxymoron An *oxymoron* is not an unintentional contradiction in terms but *a figure of speech in which contradictory terms are deliberately combined*, as in: *bitter-sweet, cruel kindness, friendly fire, jolie laide, open secret, sweet sorrow*, etc.

Pakistani names *see* **names.**

palate, pallet, palette Your *palate*, the roof of your mouth (or your capacity to appreciate food and drink), is best not confused with a *pallet*, a mattress on which you may sleep or a wooden frame for use with fork-lift trucks, still less with a *palette*, on which you may mix paints.

panacea Universal remedy. Beware of cliché usage. *See also* page 33.

parliaments Do not confuse one part of a parliament with the whole thing. The Dail is only the lower house of Ireland's parliament, as the Duma is of Russia's and the Lok Sabha is of India's.

partner is useful for those who value gender-neutrality above all else, but others may prefer *boyfriend* or *girlfriend* or even *lover*. And remember that, if you take a *partner for the Gay Gordons*, you may not end up in bed together – just as lawyers and accountants and others *in partnerships* are not necessarily fornicating, even if they are *sleeping partners*.

passive *see* **active, not passive.**

peer (noun) is one of those words beloved of sociologists and eagerly co-opted by journalists who want to make their prose seem more authoritative. A *peer* is not a *contemporary, colleague* or *counterpart* but an *equal*.

per caput is the Latin for per head. *Per capita* is the Latin for by heads; it is a term used by lawyers when distributing an inheritance among individuals, rather than among families (*per stirpes*). Unless the context demands this technical expression, never use either *per capita* or *per caput* but *per person*. *See also* **figures.**

per cent is not the same as a *percentage point*. Nothing can fall, or be devalued, by more than 100%. If something trebles, it increases by 200%. If a growth rate increases from 4% to 6%, the rate is two percentage points or 50% faster, not 2%. *See also* **figures**.

percolate means to pass *through*, not *up* or *down*.

phone (noun) is permissible, especially when preceded by *mobile*. But use sparingly, and generally prefer *telephone*.

photo Prefer *photograph*.

placenames Use English forms when they are in common use.

Andalusia	Dagestan	Munich
Archangel (not	Dnieper	Naples
Archangelsk or	Dniester (but	Nuremberg
Arkhangelsk)	Transdniestria)	Odessa
Brest	Florence	Pomerania
Brunswick	Geneva	Salonika
Cassel (not Kassel)	Genoa	Saragossa
Castile	Hanover	Saxony (and Lower
Catalonia	Leghorn	Saxony, Saxony-
Cologne	Lower Saxony	Anhalt)
Cordoba	Lucerne	Sebastopol
Corinth	Majorca	Seville
Corunna	Minorca	Zurich without an
Cracow	Minsk	umlaut

Use English rather than American – *Rockefeller Centre, Bar Harbour, Pearl Harbour* – unless the placename is part of a company's name, such as *Rockefeller Center Properties Inc.*

Europe Note that although the place is *western* (or *eastern*) *Europe*, euphony dictates that the people are *west* (or *east*) *Europeans*.

definite article Do not use the definite article before:

Krajina	Sudan
Lebanon	Transkei
Piedmont	Ukraine
Punjab	

But:

the Caucasus
the Gambia
The Hague
the Maghreb

the Netherlands
La Paz
Le Havre
Los Angeles

Abkhazia
Ajaria (not Adjaria)
Andalusia
Argentina (adj and people
  Argentine, not
  Argentinian)
Ashgabat
Azerbaijan
Baden-Württemberg
Baghdad
Bahamas (Bahamian)
Beqaa
Bermuda, Bermudian
Bophuthatswana
Bosporus (not Bosphorus)
British Columbia
Brittany, Breton
Cameroon
Cape Town
Caribbean
Catalan
Chechnya
Chernihiv
Chur
Cincinnati
Colombia (South America)
Columbia (university, District
  of)
the Comoros
Côte d'Ivoire, Ivorian
Czech Republic; Czech Lands
Dar es Salaam
Dhaka
Djibouti
Dominica (Caribbean island)

Dominican Republic (part of
  another island)
Dusseldorf (not Düsseldorf)
El Salvador, Salvadorean
Fribourg
Gaza Strip (and City)
Gettysburg
Gomel
Gothenburg
Grozny
Guantánamo
Gujarat, Gujarati
Guyana (but French Guiana)
Gweru (not Gwelo)
Hanover
Hercegovina
Hong Kong
Ingushetia
Issyk-Kul
KaNgwane
Kathmandu
Krajina
Kyiv
KwaNdebele
KwaZulu-Natal
Kwekwe (not Que Que)
Laos, Lao (not Laotian)
Ljubljana
Luhansk
Luxembourg
Lviv
Macau
Mafikeng
Mauritania
Mpumalanga (formerly
  Eastern Transvaal)

Nagorno-Karabakh
Nepal, Nepali (not Nepalese)
Nizhny Novgorod
North Rhine-Westphalia
Odessa
Ouagadougou
Philippines (the people are
    Filipinos and Filipinas)
Phnom Penh
Pittsburgh
Portugal, Portuguese
Putumayo
Pyrenees, Pyrenean
Quebec, Quebecker (but
    Parti Québécois)
Reykjavik
Rheims
Romania
Rwanda, Rwandan (not
    Rwandese)
Saragossa

St Petersburg
Salonika (not Thessaloniki)
Salzburg
São Paulo (Brazilian city)
Sindh
Srebrenica
Sri Lanka
Strasbourg
Suriname
Taipei
Tehran
Teesside
Tigray, Tigrayan
Turin
Uffizi
Uzbekistan
Valletta
Yangzi
Zepa
Zepce

some spellings

See also **countries and their inhabitants**.

plants For the spelling of the Latin names of animals, plants, etc, *see* **Latin names**.

plurals *see* **spelling**. For plural nouns, *see* **grammar and syntax**.

political correctness Avoid, if you can, giving gratuitous offence (*see* **euphemisms**): you risk losing your readers, or at least their goodwill, and therefore your arguments. But pandering to every plea for politically correct terminology may make your prose unreadable, and therefore also unread.

So strike a balance. If you judge that a group wishes to be known by a particular term, that the term is widely understood and that using any other would seem odd, old-fashioned or offensive, then use it. Context may be important: *Coloured* is a common term in South Africa for people of mixed race; it is not considered derogatory. Elsewhere it may be. Remember that both times and terms change: expressions that were in common use a few decades ago are now odious. Nothing is to be gained by casually insulting your readers.

But do not labour to avoid imaginary insults, especially if the effort does violence to the language. Some people, such as the members of the Task-force on Bias-Free Language of the Association of American University Presses, believe that *ghettoblaster* is "offensive as a stereotype of African-American culture", that it is invidious to speak of a *normal* child, that *massacre* should not be used "to refer to a successful American Indian raid or battle victory against white colonisers and invaders", and that the use of the term *cretin* is distressing. They want, they say, to avoid "victimisation" and to get "the person before the disability". The intent may be admirable, but they are unduly sensitive, often inventing slights where none exists.

An example is given by Denis Dutton in his review of the editors' advice ("What Are Editors For?", *Philosophy and Literature*, 1996, page 20). Mr Dutton points out that the origins of the word *cretin* lie in the Latin word for Christian. The term, he says, came into use as a way of acknowledging the essential humanity of a physically deformed or intellectually subnormal person. It is now used for a definable medical condition. The editors' aversion to *cretin* presumably arises from its slight similarity to *cripple*, a plain word now almost universally discarded in favour of the euphemistic *physically handicapped* or *disabled*.

As Mr Dutton points out, Thomas Bowdler provides a cautionary example. His version of Shakespeare, produced in 1818 using "judicious" paraphrase and expurgation, was designed to be read by men to their families with no one offended or embarrassed. In doing so, he gave his name to an insidious form of censorship.

Some people believe the possibility of giving offence, causing embarrassment, lowering self-esteem, reinforcing stereotypes, perpetuating prejudice, victimising, marginalising or discriminating to be more important than stating the truth, never mind the chance of doing so with any verve or panache. They are wrong. Do not self-bowdlerise your prose. You may be neither Galileo nor Salman Rushdie, but you too may sometimes be right to cause offence. Your first duty is to the truth.

he, she, they You also have a duty to grammar. The struggle to be gender-neutral rests on a misconception about gender, a grammatical convention to make words masculine, feminine or neuter. Since English is unusual in assigning few genders to nouns other than those relating to people (ships and countries are exceptions), feminists have come to argue that language should be gender-neutral.

This would be a forlorn undertaking in most tongues, and even in English it presents difficulties. It may be no tragedy that *policemen* are now almost always *police officers* and *firemen firefighters*, but to call *chairmen chairs* serves chiefly to remind everyone that the world of committees and those who make it go round are largely devoid of humour. Avoid also *chairpersons* (*chairwoman* is permissible), *humankind* and the *person in the street* – ugly expressions all.

It is no more demeaning to women to use the words *actress*, *ballerina* or *seamstress* than *goddess*, *princess* or *queen*. (Similarly, you should feel as free to separate *Siamese twins* or *welsh* on debts – at your own risk – as you would to go on a *Dutch treat*, pass through *french windows*, or play *Russian roulette*. Note, though, that you risk being *dogged* by *catty* language police.)

If you believe it is "exclusionary" or insulting to women to use *he* in a general sense, you can rephrase some sentences in the plural. Thus *Instruct the reader without lecturing him* may be put as *Instruct readers without lecturing them*. But some sentences resist this treatment: *Find a good teacher and take his advice* is not easily rendered gender-neutral. So do not be ashamed of sometimes using *man* to include *women*, or making *he* do for *she*.

And, so long as you are not insensitive in other ways, few women will be offended if you restrain yourself from putting *or she* after every *he*.

He or she which hath no stomach to this fight,
Let him or her depart; his or her passport shall be made,
And crowns for convoy put into his or her purse:
We would not die in that person's company
That fears his or her fellowship to die with us.

In some contexts, though, *she* can be a substitute for *he*:

That ever was thrall, now is he free;
That ever was small, now great is she;
Now shall God deem both thee and me
Unto His bliss if we do well.

(15th-century carol)

Avoid, above all, the sort of scrambled syntax that people adopt because they cannot bring themselves to use a singular pronoun:

We can't afford to squander anyone's talents, whatever colour their skin is.

When someone takes their own life, they leave their loved ones with an agonising legacy of guilt.

There's a child somewhere in Birmingham and all across the country and needs somebody to put their arm around them and to say: "I love you; you're a part of America." (George Bush)

See also **gender**.

populace is a term for the *common people*, not a synonym for the *population*.

positive means *definitely laid down, beyond possibility of doubt, absolute, fully convinced* or *greater than zero*. It does not mean *good*. *It was a positive meeting* probably means *It was a good, or fruitful, meeting.*

practicable, practical *Practicable* means *feasible*; *practical* means *useful*.

pre- is often unnecessary as a prefix, as in *precondition, pre-prepared, pre-cooked*. If it seems to be serving a function, try making use of a word such as already or earlier: *Here's one I cooked earlier.*

pre-owned is *second-hand*.

premier (as a noun) should be confined to the first ministers of Canadian provinces, German *Länder* and other sub-national states. Do not use it as a synonym for the prime minister of a country.

presently means *soon*, not *at present*. ("*Presently Kep opened the door of the shed, and let out Jemima Puddle-Duck.*" Beatrix Potter)

press, pressure, pressurise *Pressurise* is what you want in an aircraft, but not in an argument or encounter where persuasion is being employed, when the verb is *press*. The verb you want there is *press* (use *pressure* only as a noun).

prevaricate, procrastinate *Prevaricate* means evade the truth; *procrastinate* means delay. ("*Procrastination – or punctuality, if you are Oscar Wilde – is the thief of time.*")

pristine means *original* or *former*; it does not mean *clean*.

proactive Not a pretty word: try *active* or *energetic*.

process Some writers see their prose in industrial terms: *education* becomes an *education process*, elections an *electoral process*, development a *development process*, writing a *writing process*. If you follow this fashion, do not be surprised if readers switch off.

prodigal If you are *prodigal*, that does not mean you are *welcomed home* or *taken back without recrimination*. It means you have *squandered your patrimony*.

proofreading *see* Part 3.

propaganda (which is singular) means a *systematic effort to spread doctrine or opinions*. It is not a synonym for *lies*.

protagonist means the *chief actor* or *combatant*. If you are referring to several people, they cannot all be protagonists.

protest By all means *protest your innocence*, or *your intention to write good English*, if you are making a declaration. But if you are making a complaint or objection, you must *protest at* or *against* it.

pry Use *prise*, unless you mean *peer* or *peep*.

public schools in Britain, the places where fee-paying parents send their children; in the United States, the places where they don't.

punctuation Some guidelines on common problems.

apostrophes

1   With singular words and names that end in *s*: use the normal possessive ending *'s*:

boss's   St James's

| caucus's | Jones's |
| Delors's | Shanks's |

2   After plurals that do not end in s also use 's: *children's, Frenchmen's, media's.*

3   Use the ending s' on plurals that end in s:

Danes' bosses' Joneses'

and plural names that take a singular verb:

| Barclays' | Stewarts & Lloyds' |
| Reuters' | Salomon Brothers' |

5   Some plural nouns, although singular in other respects, such as the United States, the United Nations, the Philippines, have a plural possessive apostrophe:

Who will be the United States' next president?

6   *Lloyd's* (the insurance market): try to avoid using as a possessive; it poses an insoluble problem.

7   *Achilles heel*: the vulnerable part of the hero of the Trojan war.

8   Decades: do not put apostrophes into decades: the 1990s.

9   Phrases like *two weeks' time, four days' march, six months' leave*, also need apostrophes.

10 People:

people's = of (the) people
peoples' = of peoples

brackets   If a whole sentence is within brackets, put the full stop inside. Square brackets should be used for interpolations in direct quotations: "*Let them [the poor] eat cake.*" To use ordinary brackets implies that the words inside them were part of the original text from which you are quoting.

colons   Use a colon "to deliver the goods that have been invoiced in the preceding words" (Fowler).

They brought presents: gold, frankincense and oil at $60 a barrel.

Use a colon before a whole quoted sentence, but not before a quotation that begins in mid-sentence.

She said: "It will never work." He retorted that it had "always worked before".

commas Use commas as an aid to understanding. Too many in one sentence can be confusing.

1   It is not always necessary to put a comma after a short phrase at the start of a sentence if no natural pause exists:

When night fell he fell too.

2   But a breath, and so a comma, is needed after longer passages:

When day broke and he was able at last to see what had happened, he realised he had fallen through the roof and into the Big Brother house.

3   Use two commas, or none at all, when inserting a clause in the middle of a sentence. Thus, do not write:

Use two commas, or none at all when inserting ... or

Use two commas or none at all, when inserting ...

Similarly, two commas or none at all are needed with constructions like:

And, though he denies it, he couldn't tell a corncrake from a cornflake ...

But, when Bush comes to Shuv, he'll find it isn't a town, just a Hebrew word for Return.

4   American states: commas are essential (and often left out) after the names of American states when these are written as though they were part of an address: *Kansas City, Kansas, proves that even Kansas City needn't always be Missourible* (Ogden Nash). If the clause ends with a bracket, but is not the end of a sentence, which is not uncommon (this one does), the bracket should be followed by a comma.

5   For sense: commas can alter the sense of a sentence. To write *Mozart's 40th symphony, in G minor,* with commas indicates that this symphony was written in G minor. Without commas, *Mozart's 40th symphony in G minor* suggests he wrote 39 other symphonies in G minor.

6   Lists: with lists do not put a comma before *and* at the end of a sequence of items unless one of the items includes another *and*. Thus:

The doctor suggested an aspirin, half a grapefruit and a cup of broth. But he ordered scrambled eggs, whisky and soda, and a selection from the trolley.

7   Question-marks: do not put commas after question-marks, even when they would be separated by quotation marks:

"May I have a second helping?" he asked.

dashes   You can use dashes in pairs for parenthesis, but not more than one pair per sentence, ideally not more than one pair per paragraph.

"Use a dash to introduce an explanation, amplification, paraphrase, particularisation or correction of what immediately precedes it. Use it to gather up the subject of a long sentence. Use it to introduce a paradoxical or whimsical ending to a sentence. Do not use it as a punctuation maid-of-all-work." (Gowers)

full stops   Use plenty. They keep sentences short. This helps the reader. Do not use full stops in abbreviations or at the end of headings and subheadings.

inverted commas (quotation marks)   Use single ones only for quotations within quotations. Thus:

"When I say 'immediately', I mean some time before April," said the spokesman.

For the relative placing of quotation marks and punctuation, follow Oxford rules. Thus, if an extract ends with a full stop or question-mark, put the punctuation before the closing inverted commas.

His maxim was that "love follows laughter." In this spirit came his opening gambit: "What's the difference between a buffalo and a bison?"

If a complete sentence in quotes comes at the end of a larger sentence, the final stop should be inside the inverted commas. Thus,

The answer was, "You can't wash your hands in a buffalo." She replied, "Your jokes are execrable."

If the quotation does not include any punctuation, the closing inverted commas should precede any punctuation marks that the sentence requires. Thus:

She had already noticed that the "young man" looked about as young as the New Testament is new. Although he had been described as "fawnlike in his energy and playfulness", "a stripling with all the vigour and freshness of youth", and even as "every woman's dream toyboy", he struck his companion-to-be as the kind of old man warned of by her mother as "not safe in taxis". Where, now that she needed him, was "Mr Right"?

When a quotation is broken off and resumed after such words as *he said*, ask yourself whether it would naturally have had any punctuation at the point where it is broken off. If the answer is yes, a comma is placed within the quotation marks to represent this. Thus,

"If you'll let me see you home," he said, "I think I know where we can find a cab."

The comma after home belongs to the quotation and so comes within the inverted commas, as does the final full stop.

But if the words to be quoted are continuous, without punctuation at the point where they are broken, the comma should be outside the inverted commas. Thus:

"My bicycle", she assured him, "awaits me."

Do not use quotation marks unnecessarily:

Mr Spitzer described the British drug giant as "arrogant"; GSK accused him of "bullying".

Note that the Bible contains no quotation marks, with no consequent confusions.

question-marks Except in sentences that include a question in inverted commas, question-marks always come at the end of the sentence. Thus:

Had Zimri peace, who slew his master?

semi-colons Use them to mark a pause longer than a comma and shorter than a full stop. Don't overdo them.

Use them to distinguish phrases listed after a colon if commas will not do the job clearly. Thus:

question-marks *see* **punctuation**.

quite In America, *quite* is usually an intensifying adverb similar to *altogether*, *entirely* or *very*; in Britain, depending on the emphasis, the tone of voice and the adjective that follows, it usually means *fairly*, *moderately* or *reasonably*, and often damns with faint praise.

quotes Be sparing with quotes. Direct quotes should be used when either the speaker or what he said is surprising, or when the words he used are particularly pithy or graphic. Otherwise you can probably paraphrase him more concisely. The most pointless quote is the inconsequential remark attributed to a nameless source: *"Everyone wants to be in on the act," says one high-ranking civil servant.*

For *quotation marks* (inverted commas), *see* **punctuation**.

real Is it really necessary? When used to mean *after taking inflation into account*, it is legitimate. In other contexts (*Investors are showing real interest in the country, but Bolivians wonder if real prosperity will ever arrive*) it is often better left out.

rebut, refute *Rebut* means *repel* or *meet in argument*. *Refute*, which is stronger, means *disprove*. Neither should be used as a synonym for *deny*. "*Shakespeare never has six lines together without a fault. Perhaps you may find seven: but this does not refute my general assertion.*" (Samuel Johnson)

red and blue In Britain, colours that are associated with socialism and conservatism respectively; in the United States, colours that are associated with Republicans and Democrats respectively.

references *see* **footnotes, sources, references** in Part 3.

regrettably means *to be regretted*. Do not confuse with *regretfully*, used of someone showing regret.

relationship is a long word often better replaced by *relations*. *The two countries hope for a better relationship* means *The two countries hope for better relations*. But *relationship* is an appropriate word nowadays for two people in a close friendship.

report on not *into*.

reshuffle, resupply *Shuffle* and *supply* will do, except for British Cabinets, which are *reshuffled* from time to time.

resources, resourceful *Resourceful* is a useful word; the term *natural resources*, less satisfactory, also has its merits. Most other uses of *resource* tend to be vile. The word is entirely at home in the following sentence, taken from an advertisement placed by Skill for Business (2005): "*Sector Skills Councils ... assess what resource is already out there, and then create comprehensive deals with supply-side partners to fill skills gaps and shortages.*" Beware.

Richter scale Beloved of journalists, the Richter scale is unknown to seismologists. The strength of an earthquake is its *magnitude*, so say *an earthquake of magnitude 8.9*. *See* **earthquakes** in Part 3.

ring, wring (verbs) bells are rung; hands are wrung. Both may be seen at weddings.

Roma is the name of the people. Their language is *Romany*. Remember that *Sinti* are also gypsies.

run In countries with a presidential system you may *run* for office. In those with a parliamentary one, you *stand*.

Russian names *see* **names**.

S

same is often superfluous. If your sentence contains *on the same day that*, try *on the day that*.

scotch To *scotch* means to *disable*, not to *destroy*. ("We have scotched the snake, not killed it.") The people may also be *Scotch, Scots* or *Scottish*; choose as you like. *Scot-free* means free from payment of a fine (or punishment), not *free from Scotsmen*.

second-biggest (third-oldest, fourth-wisest, fifth-commonest, etc) Think before you write.

Apart from New York, a Bramley is the second-biggest apple in the world. Other than home-making and parenting, prostitution is the third-oldest profession. After Tom, Dick and Harriet, Henry I was the fourth-wisest fool in Christendom. Besides justice, prudence, temperance and fortitude, the fifth-commonest virtue of the Goths was punctuality.

None of these sentences should contain the ordinal (second-, third-, fourth-, fifth-, etc).

sector Try *industry* instead or, for example, *banks* instead of *banking sector*.

semi-colons *see* **punctuation.**

sensual, sensuous *Sensual* means *carnal* or *voluptuous*. *Sensuous* means pertaining to aesthetic appreciation, without any implication of lasciviousness.

sequestered, sequestrated *Sequestered* means *secluded*. *Sequestrated* means *confiscated* or *made bankrupt*.

ship A ship is feminine.

short words Use them. They are often Anglo-Saxon rather than Latin in origin. They are easy to spell and easy to understand. Thus prefer:

about to *approximately*	*plant* to *facility*
after to *following*	*set up* to *establish*
but to *however*	*show* to *demonstrate*
enough to *sufficient*	*spending* to *expenditure*
let to *permit*	*take part* to *participate*
make to *manufacture*	*use* to *utilise*

Underdeveloped countries are often better described as *poor*. *Substantive* often means *real* or *big*. "Short words are best and the old words when short are best of all." (Winston Churchill)

simplistic Prefer *simple-minded, naive*.

Singaporean names *see* **names**.

singular or plural? *see* **grammar and syntax**.

skills are turning up all over the place – in learning skills, thinking skills, teaching skills – instead of *the ability to*. *He has the skills* probably means *He can*.

skyrocketed *Rocketed*, not *skyrocketed*.

slither, sliver As a noun, *slither* is *scree*. As a verb, it means *slide*. If you mean a *slice*, the word you want is *sliver*.

sloppy writing Use words with care.

If *This door is alarmed*, does its hair stand on end? If this envelope says *Urgent: dated material*, is it really too old-fashioned to be worth reading? Is *offensive marketing* just rude salesmanship?

More serious difficulties may arise with *indicted war criminals*. As their lawyers could one day remind you, these may turn out to be *innocent people accused of war crimes*.

A *heart condition* is usually a *bad heart*. A *near miss* is probably a *near hit*. *Positive thoughts* (held by long-suffering creditors, according to *The Economist*) presumably means *optimism*, just as a *negative* report is probably a *critical* report. *Industrial action* is usually *industrial inaction, industrial disruption* or a *strike*. A *courtesy call* is generally a *sales offer* or an *uninvited visit*. A *substantially finished* bridge is an *unfinished* bridge. Someone with *high name-recognition* is *well known*. Something with *reliability problems* probably *does not work*. If yours is a *live audience*, what would a dead one be like?

And what is an *ethics violation*? An error of judgment? A crime? A moral lapse?

See also **unnecessary words.**

smart generally means *well dressed*, but *smart sanctions* and *smart weapons*, etc may be allowed as terms of art.

social security in America, *Social Security* means *pensions* and should be capitalised. Elsewhere it usually means *state benefits* more generally, which are called *welfare* in the United States.

soft is an adverb, as well as an adjective and a noun. *Softly* is also an adverb. You can speak softly and carry a big stick, but if you have a quiet voice you are *soft* – not *softly* – *spoken*.

soi-disant means *self-styled*, not *so-called*.

sources *see* **footnotes, sources, references** in Part 3.

Spanish names *see* **names.**

specific A *specific* is a *medicine*, not a *detail*.

spelling Use British English rather than American English or any other kind. Sometimes, however, this injunction will clash with the rule that people and companies should be called what they want to be called, short of festooning themselves with titles. If it does, adopt American (or Canadian or other local) spelling when it is used in the name of an American (etc) company or private organisation (*Alcan Aluminum, Carter Center, Pulverizing Services Inc, Travelers Insurance*), but not when it is used for a place or government institution (*Pearl Harbour, Department of Defence, Department of Labour*). The principle behind this ruling is that placenames are habitually changed from foreign languages into English: *Deutschland* becomes *Germany, München Munich, Torino Turin*, etc. And to respect the local spelling of government institutions would present difficulties: a sentence containing both the *Department of Labor* and the *secretary of labour*, or the *Defense Department* and the *need for a strong defence*, would look unduly odd. That oddity will arise nonetheless if you have to explain that *Rockefeller Center Properties is in charge of Rockefeller Centre*, but with luck that will not happen too often. *See* **countries and their inhabitants, placenames**.

The Australian *Labor Party* should be spelt without a *u* not only because it is not a government institution but also because the Australians spell it that way, even though they spell *labour* as the British do.

s spelling Use *-ise, -isation* (*realise, organisation*) throughout. But please do not *hospitalise*.

common problems

abattoir
abut, abutted, abutting
accommodate
acknowledgment
acquittal, acquitted, acquitting
adrenalin
adviser, advisory
aeon
aeroplane
aesthetic
aficionado
Afrikaans (the language), Afrikaner (the person)
ageing (but caging, paging, raging, waging)
agri-business (not agro-business)
aircraft, airliner
al-Qaeda
amiable
amid (not amidst)
amok (not amuck)
among (not amongst)
annex (verb), annexe (noun)
antecedent
appal, appals, appalling, appalled
aqueduct
aquifer
arbitrager
artefact
asinine
balk (not baulk)
balloted, balloting
bandanna
bandwagon
battalion
bellwether
benefiting, benefited
biased
billeting, billeted
blanketing, blanketed
block (never bloc)
blowzy (not blousy)
bogey (bogie is on a locomotive)
borsch
braggadocio
bused, busing (keep bussing for kissing)
by-election, bypass, by-product, bylaw, byword
bye (in sport)
caesium

cannon (gun), canon (standard, criterion, clergyman)
cappuccino
carcass
chancy
channelling, channelled
checking account (spell it thus when explaining to Americans a current account, which is to be preferred)
choosy
cipher
clubable (coined, and spelled thus, by Dr Johnson)
colour, colouring, colourist
combating, combated
commemorate
connection
consensus
cooled, cooler, coolly
coruscate
cosseted, cosseting
council, counsel (two different things; check sense)
defendant
dependant (person), dependent (adj)
depository (unless referring to American depositary receipts)
desiccate, desiccation
detente (not détente)
dexterous (not dextrous)
disk (in a computer context), otherwise disc (including compact disc)
dispatch (not despatch)
dispel, dispelling
distil, distiller

divergences
douse
doveish
dowse
dryer, dryly
dwelt
dyeing (colour)
dyke
ecstasy
embarrass (but harass)
encyclopedia
enroll, enrolment
ensure (make certain), insure (against risks)
enthrall
extrovert
farther (distance), further (additional)
favour, favourable
ferreted
fetus (not foetus, misformed from the Latin fetus)
field-marshal (soldier), Marshall Field's (Chicago department store)
Filipino, Filipina (person), Philippine (adj of the Philippines)
filleting, filleted
focused, focusing
forbear (abstain), forebear (ancestor)
forbid, forbade
foreboding
foreclose
forefather
forestall
forewarn
forgather
forgo (do without), forego (precede)
forsake

forswear, forsworn
fuelled
-ful, not -full (thus armful, bathful, handful, etc)
fulfil, fulfilling
fullness
fulsome
funnelling, funnelled
furore
gelatine
glamour, glamorous
gram (not gramme)
guerrilla
Gurkha
gypsy
haj
hallo (not hello)
harass (but embarrass)
hiccup (not hiccough)
honour, honourable
hotch-potch
humour, humorist, humorous
hurrah (not hooray)
idiosyncrasy
impostor
incur, incurring
inquire, inquiry (not enquire, enquiry)
install, instalment, installation
instil, instilling
intransigent
jail (not gaol)
jewellery (not jewelry)
jihad
judgment
kilogram or kilo (not kilogramme)
labelling, labelled
laissez-faire
lama (priest), llama (beast)

lambast (not lambaste)
leukaemia
levelled
libelling, libelled
licence (noun), license (verb)
linchpin, lynch law
liquefy
literal
littoral (shore)
loth (reluctant), loathe (hate), loathsome
low-tech
manilla envelope, but Manila, capital of the Philippines
manoeuvre, manoeuvring
marshal (noun and verb), marshalled
medieval
mêlée
meter (a measuring tool), metre (metric measure, meter in American)
mileage
millennium, but millenarian
minuscule
modelling, modelled
mould
Muslim (not Moslem)
naivety
'Ndrangheta
nonplussed
nought (for numerals), otherwise naught
obbligato
optics (optician, etc) ophthalmic (ophthalmology, etc)
paediatric, paediatrician
panel, panelled
parallel, paralleled
pastime

phoney (not phony)
piggyback (not pickaback)
plummeted, plummeting
practice (noun), practise (verb)
praesidium (not presidium)
predilection
preferred (preferring, but proffered)
preventive (not preventative)
pricey
primeval
principal (head, loan; or adj), principle (abstract noun)
proffered (proffering, but preferred)
profited
prophecy (noun), prophesy (verb)
protester
Pushtu, Pushtun
pygmy
pzazz
queuing
rack, racked, racking (as in racked with pain, nerve-racking)
racket
rankle
rarefy
razzmatazz
recur, recurrent, recurring
restaurateur
resuscitate
rhythm
rivet (riveted, riveter, riveting)
ropy
rottweiler
sacrilegious
sanatorium
savannah

seize
shaky
sharia
shenanigans
Shia (noun and adj), Shias, Shiism
shibboleth
Sibylline
siege
sieve
siphon (not syphon)
skulduggery
smelt
smidgen (not smidgeon)
smoky
smooth (both noun and verb)
snigger (not snicker)
sobriquet
somersault
soothe
soyabean
specialty (only in context of medicine, steel and chemicals), otherwise speciality
sphinx
spoilt
stanch (verb)
staunch (adj)
storey (floor)
supersede
Sunni, Sunnis
swap (not swop)
swathe
synonym
Tatar (not Tartar)
taoiseach (but prefer prime minister, or leader)
threshold
titbits
titillate
tonton-macoutes

tormentor
trade union, trade unions
  (but Trades Union
  Congress)
transferred, transferring
travelled
tricolor
trouper (as in old trouper)
tsar
tyre
untrammelled
vaccinate

vacillate
vermilion
wacky
wagon (not waggon)
weasel, weaselly
while not whilst
wiggle (not wriggle) room
wilful
withhold
yarmulke (prefer to *kippah*)
yogurt

-able

debatable
dispensable
disputable
forgivable
imaginable
implacable

indescribable
indictable
indispensable
indistinguishable
lovable
movable

salable (but prefer sellable)
tradable
unmistakable
unshakable
unusable
usable

-eable

bridgeable
changeable
knowledgeable
likeable

manageable
rateable
serviceable
sizeable

traceable
unenforceable
unpronounceable

-ible

accessible
convertible
digestible

inadmissible
indestructible
investible

irresistible
permissible
submersible

plurals No rules here. The spelling of the following plurals may be
   decided by either practice or derivation.

-a

consortia
corrigenda
data
media

memoranda
millennia
phenomena
quanta

sanatoria
spectra
strata

-ae

amoebae	formulae
antennae	lacunae

-eaus

bureaus	plateaus

-eaux

chateaux	tableaux

-fs

dwarfs	still-lifes
roofs	turfs

-i

alumni	nuclei	termini
bacilli	stimuli	

-oes

archipelagoes	haloes	salvoes
buffaloes	heroes	tomatoes
cargoes	innuendoes	tornadoes
desperadoes	mementoes	torpedoes
dominoes	mosquitoes	vetoes
echoes	mottoes	volcanoes
embargoes	noes	
frescoes	potatoes	

-os

albinos	Eskimos	manifestos
armadillos	falsettos	memos
calicos	fandangos	mulattos
casinos	fiascos	neutrinos
commandos	flamingos	oratorios
demos	folios	peccadillos
dynamos	ghettos	pianos
egos	impresarios	placebos
embryos	librettos	provisos

quangos
radios
silos
solos

sopranos
stilettos
studios

virtuosos
weirdos
zeros

-s

agendas

-ums

conundrums
crematoriums
curriculums
forums

moratoriums
nostrums
quorums
referendums

stadiums
symposiums
ultimatums
vacuums

-uses

buses
caucuses
circuses
fetuses

focuses
geniuses
prospectuses

-ves

hooves

scarves

wharves

Note: *indexes* (of books), but *indices* (indicators, index numbers); *appendices* (supplements), but *appendixes* (anatomical organs).

split infinitives see **syntax.**

stanch, staunch *Stanch* the flow, though the man be *staunch* (stout). The distinction is useful, if bogus (since both words derive from the same old-French *estancher*).

stationary, stationery *Stationary* is still; *stationery* is writing paper, envelopes, etc.

stentorian, stertorous *Stentorian* means *loud* (like the voice of Stentor, a warrior in the Trojan war). *Stertorous* means *characterised by a snoring sound* (from *sterto*, snore).

straight, strait *Straight* means *direct* or *uncurved; strait* means *narrow* or *tight*. The *strait-laced* tend to be *straight-faced*. *Straits* are narrow bodies of water between bits of land.

strategy, strategic *Strategy* may sometimes have some merit, especially in military contexts, as a contrast to *tactics*. But *strategic* is usually meaningless except to tell you that the writer is pompous and is trying to invest something with a seriousness it does not deserve.

-style Avoid *German-style supervisory boards, an EU-style rotating presidency*, etc. Explain what you mean.

subcontract If you engage someone to do something, you are *contracting* the job to him; only if he then asks someone else to do it is the job *subcontracted*.

swear words Avoid them, unless they convey something genuinely helpful or interesting to the reader (eg, you are quoting someone). Usually, they will annoy rather than shock. But if you do use them, spell them out in full, without asterisks.

Swiss names *see* **names.**

syntax *see* **grammar and syntax.**

systemic, systematic *Systemic* means *relating to a system or body as a whole*. *Systematic* means *according to system, methodical* or *intentional*.

table Avoid *table* as a transitive verb. In Britain to *table* means to bring something forward for action, and should be kept to committees. In America it sometimes means exactly the opposite.

target Not so long ago *target* was almost unknown as a verb, except when used to mean *provide with a shield*. Now it turns up almost everywhere, even though *aim* or *direct* would often serve as well.

terrorist Use with care, preferably only to mean *someone who uses terror as an organised system of intimidation*.
Prefer *suspected terrorists* to *terrorist suspects*.

testament, testimony A *testament* is a will; *testimony* is evidence. It is *testimony to the poor teaching of English that journalists habitually write testament instead*.

the Occasionally, the use of the definite article may be optional: *Maximilien Robespierre, the leader of the Committee of Public Safety*, is preferable to *Maximilien Robespierre, leader of the Committee of Public Safety*, but in this context the *the* after *Robespierre* is not essential. However, *Given that leaders of mainstream left and right parties* (The Economist, April 16th 2005) means something different from *Given that the leaders of both mainstream left and right parties*. Likewise, *If polls are right* means something different from *If the polls are right* (same issue). *They include freedom to set low flat taxes* (same issue) is similarly, if subtly, different from *They include the freedom to set low flat taxes*. In each of these examples the crucial *the* was left out. *See also* **a or the**.

there is, there are Often unnecessary. *There are three issues facing the prime minister* is better as *Three issues face the prime minister*.

throe, throw *Throe* is a *spasm* or *pang* (and is usually in the plural). *Throw* is to *cast* or *hurl through the air. Last throws* may be all right on the cricket pitch, but *last throes* are more likely on the battlefield.

ticket, platform, manifesto The *ticket* lists the names of the candidates for a particular party (so if you *split your ticket* you vote for, eg, a Republican for president and a Democrat for Congress). The *platform* is the statement of basic principles (*planks*) put forward by an American party, usually at its pre-election convention. It is thus akin to a British party's *manifesto*, which sets out the party's policies.

times Take care. *Three times more than X is four times as much as X.*

titles The overriding principle is to treat people with respect. That usually means giving them the title they themselves adopt. But some titles are ugly (Ms), some misleading (all Italian graduates are Dr), and some tiresomely long (Mr Dr Dr Federal Sanitary-Inspector Schmidt). Do not therefore indulge people's self-importance unless it would seem insulting not to.

Do not use Mr, Mrs, Miss, Ms or Dr on first mention. Plain *George Bush, Tony Blair* or other appropriate combination of first name and surname will do. But thereafter the names of all living people should be preceded by Mr, Mrs, Miss or some other title. Serving soldiers, sailors, airmen, etc should be given their title on first and subsequent mentions. Those (such as Colin Powell, but not Pervez Musharraf) who cast aside their uniforms for civvy street become plain Mr (or whatever). Governor X, President Y, the Rev John Z may be Mr, Mrs or Miss on second mention.

On first mention use forename and surname; then drop the forename (unless there are two people with the same surname mentioned).

Jacques Chirac, then *Mr Chirac*

1   Avoid nicknames and diminutives unless the person is always known (or prefers to be known) by one:

Tony Blair   Dick Cheney   Bill Emmott   Newt Gingrich

2   Avoid the habit of joining office and name: *Prime Minister Blair, Budget Commissioner Schreyer*. But *Chancellor Schröder* is permissible.

3   Knights, dames, princes, kings, etc should have their titles on first and subsequent mentions.

Many peers are, however, better known by their former names. Those like Paddy Ashdown, Laurence Olivier and Helena Kennedy can be given their familiar names on first mention. After that, they should be called by their titles. Life peeresses may be called *Lady*, not *Baroness*, just as barons are called *Lord*. (*See* **British titles** below.)

4   If you use a title, get it right. *Rear-Admiral* Jones should not, at least on first mention, be called *Admiral* Jones.

5   Titles are not necessary in headings or captions, although surnames are: no *Kens, Tonys, Gordons, Newts*, etc. Sometimes they can also be dispensed with for athletes and pop stars, if titles would make them seem more ridiculous than dignified.

6   The dead: no titles, except those whom you are writing about because they have just died. *Dr Johnson* and *Mr Gladstone* are also permissible.

7   *Ms* is permissible though ugly. Avoid it if you can. To call a woman *Miss* is not to imply that she is unmarried, merely that she goes by her maiden name. Married women who are known by their maiden names – eg, Aung San Suu Kyi, Benazir Bhutto, Jane Fonda – are therefore Miss, unless they have made it clear that they want to be called something else.

8   Foreign titles: take care. Malaysian titles are so confusing that it may be wise to dispense with them altogether. Do not call *Tunku Razaleigh Hamzah Mr Razaleigh Hamzah*; if you are not giving him his Tunku, refer to him, on each mention, as *Razaleigh Hamzah*. Avoid *Mr Tunku Razaleigh Hamza*.

9   Dr: use *Dr* only for qualified medical people, unless the correct alternative is not known or it would seem perverse to use *Mr*. And try to keep *Professor* for those who hold chairs, not just a university job or an inflated ego.

10   Middle initials: omit. You may have to distinguish between *George Bush junior* and *George Bush senior*, but nobody will imagine that the *Lyndon Johnson* you are writing about is *Lyndon A. Johnson* or *Lyndon C. Johnson*.

11   Some titles serve as names, and therefore have initial capitals, though are also descriptions: *the Archbishop of Canterbury*,

the *Emir of Kuwait, the Shah of Iran.* If you want to describe the office rather than the individual, use lower case: *The next archbishop of Canterbury will be a woman.* Use lower case in references simply to the *archbishop, the emir, the shah: The Duchess of Scunthorpe was in her finery, but the duke wore jeans.*

British titles Long incomprehensible to all foreigners and most Britons, British titles and forms of address now seem just as confusing to those who hold them. Snobbery, embarrassment and obscurity make it difficult to know whether to write Mrs Thatcher, Mrs Margaret Thatcher, Lady Thatcher, Baroness Thatcher, Lady Margaret Thatcher or Baroness Margaret Thatcher. Properly, she is Margaret, Baroness Thatcher, but on first mention the following are preferable: *Margaret Thatcher* or *Lady Thatcher.* On subsequent mentions, *Lady Thatcher* is fine. If the context is historical, *Margaret Thatcher* and thereafter *Mrs (now Lady) Thatcher.*

On first mention all *viscounts, earls, marquesses, dukes* etc should be given their titles (shorn of all Right Honourables, etc). Thereafter they can be plain *Lord* (except for dukes). *Barons,* a category that includes all *life peers,* can always be called *Lord.* The full names of *knights* should be spelled out on first mention. Thereafter they become *Sir Firstnameonly.*

clerical titles Ordained clerics should be given their proper titles, though not their full honorifics (no need for His Holiness, His Eminence, the Right Reverend, etc). But:

the *Rev Michael Wall* (thereafter *Mr Wall*)
Father Ted (Father Ted)
Bishop Kevin Auckland (Bishop Auckland)
Archbishop Desmond Tutu (Archbishop Tutu)

Imams, muftis, ayatollahs, rabbis, gurus, etc should be given an appropriate title if they use one, and it should be repeated on second and subsequent mentions, so:

Ayatollah Hossein-Ali Montazeri (Ayatollah Montazeri)
Rabbi Lionel Bloom (Rabbi Bloom)
Sri Sri Ravi Shankar (Sri Sri Ravi Shankar)

to or and? To *try and end the killing* does not mean the same as *to try to end the killing.*

total is all right as a noun, but as a verb prefer *amount to* or *add up to*.

transpire means *exhale*, not *happen*, *occur* or *turn out*.

transportation in America, a means of getting from A to B; in Britain, a means of getting rid of convicts.

tribe Regarded as politically incorrect in some circles, *tribe* is widely used in Africa and other places. It should not be regarded as derogatory and is often preferable to *ethnic group*. *See also* **ethnic groups, political correctness**.

trillion A thousand billion (*see* **figures**).

trooper, trouper An old trooper is an old *cavalry soldier* (supposedly good at swearing), old *private soldier* in a tank regiment, or old *mounted policeman*. An old trouper is an old *member of a theatrical company*, or perhaps a *good sort*.

Turk, Turkic, Turkmen, Turkoman, etc *see* **countries and their inhabitants**.

twinkle, twinkling *In the twinkling of an eye* means *in a very short time*. *Before he was even a twinkle in his father's eye* means *Before* (perhaps *just before*) *he was conceived*. So, more loosely, *Before the Model T was even a twinkle in Henry Ford's eye* could mean *Before Henry Ford was even thinking about a mass-produced car*. *Before the internet was even a twinkle in Al Gore's eyes*, however, suggests *Al Gore invented the internet*.

Ukrainian names *see* **names.**

underprivileged Since a privilege is a special favour or advantage, it is by definition not something to which everyone is entitled. So *underprivileged*, by implying the right to privileges for all, is not just ugly jargon but also nonsense.

unique do not use it unless it is true. Unique means, literally, of which there is only one.

unlike should not be followed by *in*. Like *like*, *unlike* governs nouns and pronouns, not verbs and clauses.

unnecessary words Some words add nothing but length to your prose. Use adjectives to make your meaning more precise and be cautious of those you find yourself using to make it more emphatic. The word *very* is a case in point. If it occurs in a sentence you have written, try leaving it out and see whether the meaning is changed. *The omens were good* may have more force than *The omens were very good*.
　　Avoid:

strike action (strike will do)
cutbacks (cuts)
track record (record)
wilderness area (usually either a wilderness or a wild area)
large-scale (big)
the policymaking process (policymaking)
sale events (sales)
weather conditions (weather)

This time around means *This time*, just as *any time soon* means *soon*. And *at this moment in time* means *now* or *at present*.
　　Shoot off, or rather shoot, as many prepositions after verbs as possible. Thus:

Companies can be *bought* and *sold* rather than *bought up* and *sold off*.

Budgets may be *cut* rather than *cut back*.

Plots can be *hatched* but not *hatched up*.

Organisations should be *headed by* rather than *headed up by* chairmen.

Markets should be *freed*, rather than *freed up*.

Children can be *sent* to bed rather than *sent off* to bed – though if they are to *sit up* they must first *sit down*.

Pre-prepared just means *prepared*.

Certain words are often redundant:

The leader of the *so-called* Front for a Free Freedonia is the leader of the Front for a Free Freedonia.

A *top politician* or *top priority* is usually just a *politician* or a *priority*.

A *major speech* is usually just a *speech*.

Most probably and *most especially* are *probably* and *especially*.

the fact that can often be shortened to *that* (*That I did not do so was a self-indulgence*).

Loans to the *industrial and agricultural sectors* are just *loans to industry and farming*.

Member states or *member countries* of the EU may simply be referred to as *members*.

In general, be concise. Try to be economical in your account or argument ("*The best way to be boring is to leave nothing out*" – Voltaire). Similarly, try to be economical with words – but not with the truth. "*As a general rule, run your pen through every other word you have written; you have no idea what vigour it will give to your style*" (Sydney Smith). Raymond Mortimer put it even more crisply when commenting about Susan Sontag: "*Her journalism, like a diamond, will sparkle more if it is cut.*"

See also **community, jargon, sloppy writing**.

use and abuse are much used and abused. You *take* drugs, not *use* them (Does he use sugar?). And *drug abuse* is just *drug taking*, as is *substance abuse*, unless it is *glue sniffing* or *bun throwing*.

venerable means *worthy of reverence*. It is not a synonym for *old*.

venues Avoid them. Try *places*.

verbal Every agreement, except the nod-and-wink variety, is *verbal*. If you mean one that was not written down, describe it as *oral*.

viable means *capable of living*. Do not apply it to things like railway lines. *Economically viable* means *profitable*.

Vietnamese names *see* **names**.

warn is transitive, so you must either *give warning* or *warn somebody*.

wars Prefer lower case for the names of wars:

American civil war
cold war
Gulf war
war of the Spanish succession
the war of Jenkins' ear

But these are exceptions:

the Thirty Years War
the War of Independence
the Wars of the Roses

Write:

the first world war or *the 1914-18 war*, not *world war one, I* or *1*
the second world war or *the 1939-45 war*, not *world war two, II* or *2*

Post-war and *pre-war* are hyphenated.

which and that *Which* informs, *that* defines. *This is the house that Jack built.* But *This house, which Jack built, is now falling down.* Americans tend to be fussy about making a distinction between *which* and *that*. Good writers of British English are less fastidious. ("*We have left undone those things which we ought to have done.*")

while is best used temporally. Do not use it in place of *although* or *whereas*.

who, whom *Who* is one of the few words in English that differs in the accusative (objective) case, when it becomes *whom*, often throwing native English-speakers into a fizzle.

In the sentence *This is the man who can win the support of most Tory MPs*, the word you want is *who*, since *who* is the subject of the relative clause. It remains the subject, and therefore also *who*, in the sentence *This is the man who she believes (or says or insists etc)* can win the support of most Tory MPs. That becomes clearer if the sentence is punctuated thus: *This is the man who, she believes (or says or insists etc), can win the support of most Tory MPs.*

However, in the sentence *This is the man whom most Tory MPs can support*, the word in question is *whom* because the subject of the relative clause has become *most Tory MPs*. *Whom* is also necessary in the sentence *This is the man whom she believes to be able to win the support of most Tory MPs*. This is because the verb *believe* is here being used as a transitive verb, when it must be followed by an infinitive. If, however, the word *insists* were used instead of *believes*, the sentence could not be similarly changed, because the verb *insist* cannot be used transitively.

wrack is an old word meaning *vengeance*, *punishment* or *wreckage* (as in *wrack and ruin*). It can also be *seaweed*. And as a verb it can mean *ruin*. It is not an instrument of torture or a receptacle for toast: that is *rack*. Hence *racked with pain*, *by war*, *drought*, etc. *Rack your brains* – unless they be *wracked*.

part 2

American and British English

The differences between English as written and spoken in America and English as used in Britain are considerable, as is the potential for misunderstanding, even offence, when using words or phrases that are unfamiliar or mean something else on the other side of the Atlantic. This section highlights important differences between American and British English syntax and punctuation, spelling and usage.

A number of subjects call for detailed, specialised guidance beyond the scope of this book, though some of the vocabulary is dealt with here. These include food and cookery (different names for ingredients and equipment; different systems of measurement); medicine and health care (different professional titles, drug names, therapies); human anatomy; and gardening (different seasons and plants). Many crafts and hobbies also use different terms for equipment, materials and techniques. *See also* **Americanisms** in Part 1.

Grammar and syntax

Written American English tends to be more declarative than its British counterpart, and adverbs and some modifying phrases are frequently positioned differently. For example, British English may say: "*As well as going shopping, we went to the park.*" American English would turn the opening phrase around: "*We went to the park as well as going shopping*", or would begin the sentence with "*In addition to*". British English also tends to use more modifying phrases, while American English prefers to go with simpler sentence structure.

In British English doctors and lawyers are to be found *in* Harley Street or Wall Street, not *on* it. And they rest from their labours *at* weekends, not *on* them. During the week their children are *at* school, not *in* it.

Words may also be inserted or omitted in some standard phrases. British English goes *to hospital*, American English *to the hospital*. British English chooses *one or other thing*; American English chooses *one thing or the other*.

Punctuation

colons and capitals When a colon precedes a full sentence or question rather than a phrase, Americans sometimes follow the colon with a capital letter. *The mystery was explained: The impala on the menu was an animal, not a car.* The British would treat this as a simple sentence with only an initial capital letter.

commas in lists The use of a comma before the final *and* in a list is called the serial or Oxford comma: *eggs, bacon, potatoes, and cheese.* Most American writers and publishers use the serial comma; most British writers and publishers use the serial comma only when necessary to avoid ambiguity: *eggs, bacon, potatoes and cheese* but *The musicals were by Rodgers and Hammerstein, Sondheim, and Lerner and Lowe.*

full stops (periods) The American convention is to use full stops (periods) at the end of almost all abbreviations and contractions. The British convention is to use full stops after abbreviations – eg, *abbr., adj., co.* – but not after contractions – eg, *Dr, Mr, Mrs, St.*

hyphens American English is far readier than British English to accept compound words. In particular, many nouns made of two separate nouns are spelt as one word in American English, while in British English they either remain separate or are joined by a hyphen: eg, *applesauce, highborn* (hyphenated in British English). British English also tends, more than American English, to use hyphens as pronunciation aids, to separate repeated vowels in words such as *pre-empt* and *re-examine*, and to join some prefixes to nouns – eg, *pseudo-science.* The disappearance of the hyphen in these usages is also subject to change more rapidly in American English than British English, as new editions of dictionaries reflect.

British English usually uses the hyphen in compound adjectives or adjectival phrases that precede the noun, which promotes consistency, whereas American English omits it when the writer or publisher thinks that there is no risk of ambiguity or hesitation in understanding on the part of the reader, a subjective view. Thus, American English accepts *emerald green paint* but expects *blue-green algae*; British English employs the hyphen in both cases.

American English determines word breaks at the ends of justified lines of type according to pronunciation. Traditional British English breaks words according to etymology first, and pronunciation where there is no clear etymological guide. Because pronunciation often differs on opposite sides of the Atlantic, so does the position of the word break, eg, *dem-ocracy* and *phys-ical* in British English, and *democ-racy* and *physi-cal* in American English. Unfortunately, in practice word-processing software often dictates where words break, but for those who care about such things, word-division dictionaries exist for both forms of English.

quotation marks In American publications and those of some Commonwealth countries, and also international publications like *The Economist*, the convention is to use double quotation marks, reserving single quotation marks for quotes within quotes. In most British publications (excluding *The Economist*), the convention is the reverse: single quotation marks are used first, then double.

With other punctuation the relative position of quotation marks and other punctuation also differs. The British convention is to place such punctuation according to sense. The American convention is simpler but less logical: all commas and full stops precede the final quotation mark (or, if there is a quote within a quote, the first final quotation mark). Other punctuation – colons, semi-colons, question and exclamation marks – is placed according to sense. The following examples illustrate these differences.

British

The words on the magazine's cover, 'The link between coffee and cholesterol', caught his eye.

'You're eating too much,' she told him. 'You'll soon look like your father.'

'Have you seen this article, "The link between coffee and cholesterol"?' he asked.

'It was as if', he explained, 'I had swallowed a toad, and it kept croaking "ribbut, ribbut", from deep in my belly.'

She particularly enjoyed the article 'Looking for the "New Man"'.

American

The words on the magazine's cover, "The link between coffee and cholesterol," caught his eye.

"You're eating too much," she told him. "You'll soon look like your father."

"Have you seen this article, 'The link between coffee and cholesterol'?" he asked.

"It was as if," he explained, "I had swallowed a toad, and it kept croaking 'ribbut, ribbut,' from deep in my stomach."

She particularly enjoyed the article "Looking for the 'New Man.'"

Spelling

Some words are spelt differently in American and British English. The spellings are sufficiently similar to identify the word, but the unfamiliar form may still disturb the reader. If writing for an international audience, it may be better to use a synonym than to take this risk, although sometimes it cannot be avoided.

American English is more obviously phonetic than British English. The word *cosy* becomes *cozy*, *aesthetic* becomes *esthetic*, *sizeable* becomes *sizable*, *arbour* becomes *arbor*, *theatre* becomes *theater*.

Main spelling differences

-ae/-oe Although it is now common in British English to write *medieval* rather than *mediaeval*, other words – often scientific terms such as *aeon*, *diarrhoea*, *anaesthetic*, *gynaecology*, *homoeopathy* – retain their classical composite vowel. In American English, the composite vowel is replaced by a single *e*; thus, *eon*, *diarrhea*, *anesthetic*, *gynecology*, *homeopathy*.

-ce/-se In British English, the verb that relates to a noun ending in *-ce* is sometimes given the ending *-se*; thus, *advice* (noun), *advise* (verb), *device/devise*, *licence/license*, *practice/practise*. In the first two instances, the spelling change is accompanied by a slight change in the sound of the word; but in the other two instances, noun and verb are pronounced the same way, and American English spelling reflects this, by using the same spelling: thus, *license* and *practice*. It also extends the use of *-se* to other nouns that in British English are spelt *-ce*: thus, *defense*, *offense*, *pretense*.

-e/-ue The final silent *e* or *ue* of several words is omitted in American English but retained in British English: thus, *analog/analogue*, *ax/axe*, *catalog/catalogue*.

-eable/-able The silent *e*, created when forming some adjectives with this suffix, is more often omitted in American English; thus, *likeable* is spelt *likable*, *unshakeable* is spelt *unshakable*. But the *e* is sometimes retained in American English where it affects the sound of the preceding consonant; thus, *traceable* and *manageable*.

-ize/-ise The American convention is to spell with z many words that some British people and publishers (including *The Economist*) spell with s. The z spelling is, of course, also a correct British form. Remember, though, that some words must end in *-ise*, whichever spelling convention is being followed. These include:

advertise	despise	incise
advise	devise	merchandise
apprise	disguise	premise
arise	emprise	prise
chastise	enfranchise	revise
circumcise	excise	supervise
comprise	exercise	surmise
compromise	franchise	surprise
demise	improvise	televise

Words with the ending -*lyse* in British English, such as *analyse* and *paralyse*, are spelt -*lyze* in American English.

-ll/-l In British English, when words ending in the consonant *l* are given a suffix beginning with a vowel (eg, the suffixes -*able*, -*ed*, -*ing*, -*ous*, -*y*), the *l* is doubled; thus, *annul/annulled*, *model/modelling*, *quarrel/quarrelling*, *rebel/rebellious*, *wool/woolly*. This is inconsistent with the general rule in British English that the final consonant is doubled before the suffix only when the preceding vowel carries the main stress: thus, the word *regret* becomes *regretted*, or *regrettable*; but the word *billet* becomes *billeted*. American English mostly does not have this inconsistency. So if the stress does not fall on the preceding vowel, the *l* is not doubled: thus, *model/modeling*, *travel/traveler*; but *annul/annulled*.

Several words that end in a single *l* in British English – eg, *appal*, *fulfil* – take a double *ll* in American English. In British English the *l* stays single when the word takes a suffix beginning with a consonant (eg, the suffixes -*ful*, -*fully*, -*ment*): thus, *fulfil/fulfilment*. Words ending in -*ll* usually lose one *l* when taking one of these suffixes: thus, *skill/skilful*, *will/wilfully*. In American English, words ending in -*ll* usually remain intact, whatever the suffix: thus, *skill/skillful*, *will/willfully*.

-m/-mme American English tends to use the shorter form of ending, thus *program* and *gram*, and British English tends to use the longer: *programme* and *gramme*. Software *program* is always spelt thus.

-our/-or Most British English words ending in -*our* – *ardour*, *behaviour*, *candour*, *demeanour*, *favour*, *valour* and the like – lose the *u* in American English: thus, *ardor*, *candor*, etc.

-re/-er Most British English words ending in *-re* – such as *centre*, *fibre*, *metre*, *theatre* – end in *-er* in American English: thus, *center*, *fiber*, etc. Exceptions include: *acre*, *cadre*, *lucre*, *massacre*, *mediocre*, *ogre*.

-t/-ed Although this seems to be a mere difference in spelling the past tense of some verbs, it is really a different form; *see* 'Verbs: past tenses' below.

Other common spelling differences

British	American
aluminium	aluminum
apophthegm	apothegm
behove	behoove
chequered	checkered (pattern)
draught	draft
dyke	dike
eyrie	aerie
furore	furor
grey	gray
kerb/kerbside	curb/curbside
manoeuvre/manoeuvrable	maneuver/maneuverable
mould/moulder/moult	mold/molder/molt
moustache	mustache
plough	plow
podgy	pudgy
polythene	polyethylene
rumbustious	rambunctious
specialist shop	specialty shop
speciality (but specialty for medicine, steel and chemicals)	specialty
sulphur(ous)	sulfur(ous)
titbit	tidbit
towards	toward
tyre	tire

Usage

exclusivity What is familiar in one culture may be entirely alien in another. British English exploits terms and phrases borrowed from the game of cricket; American English uses baseball terms. Anyone writing for readers in both markets uses either set of

terms at his peril. Do not make references or assumptions that
are geographically exclusive, for example by specifying months
or seasons when referring to seasonal patterns, by using north
or south to imply a type of climate, or by making geographical
references that give a state's name followed by USA, as in
Wyoming, USA. You can help to avoid confusion: *Cambridge,
England*; *Cambridge, MA*.

race and sex The difficulties that arise in Europe with references to
race and sex (see **ethnic groups, political correctness** in Part 1)
are even greater in America. When referring to Americans whose
ancestors came from Africa, many people use *African-American*
or *Afro-American* rather than *black*. It is unacceptable to refer to
American Indians as *red*; they are often called *Native Americans*. It
can also cause offence to describe the original inhabitants of the
lands stretching from Greenland to Alaska as *Eskimos*; this was
a corruption of a Cree word meaning *raw-flesh eater*. The people
themselves have at least three major tribal groupings. Alaska
natives are usually called *native Americans* in Alaska. *Inuit* should
be used only to refer to people of that tribe.

It is unwise to describe an adult African-American female as a
girl, and offensive to address or refer to an adult African-American
man as a *boy*.

units of measurement In British publications measurements are now
largely expressed in SI units (the modern form of metric units),
although imperial measures are still used in certain contexts. In
American publications measurements may be expressed in SI units
but imperial units are still more common.

Although the British imperial and American standard
measures are usually identical, there are some important
exceptions, eg, the number of fluid ounces in a pint: 16 in the
American system and 20 in the British. Some measures are
peculiar to one or other national system, particularly units of mass
relating to agriculture. *See also* **measures** in Part 3.

verbs: past tenses *-t/-ed* Both forms of ending are acceptable in British
English, but the *-t* form is dominant – *burnt, learnt, spelt* – whereas
American English uses *-ed*: *burned, learned, spelled*. Contrarily,
British English uses *-ed* for the past tense and past participle of
certain verbs – *quitted, sweated* – while American English uses the
infinitive spelling – *quit, sweat*. Some verbs have a different form

of past tense and past participle, eg, the past tense of *dive* is *dived* in British English, but *dove* in American English. Although *loaned* is still sometimes used as the past tense of *lend* in American English, it is not standard.

Vocabulary

Sometimes the same word has taken on different meanings on the two sides of the Atlantic, creating an opportunity for misunderstanding. The word *homely*, for example, means *simple* or *informal* in British English, but *plain* or *unattractive* in American English.

This also applies to figures of speech. *It went like a bomb* in British English means it was a great success; *it bombed* in American English means it was a disaster. *To table* something in British English means to bring it forward for action; but in American English it means the opposite, i.e. *to shelve*.

One writer's slang is another's lively use of words; formal language to one is pomposity to another. This is the trickiest area to negotiate when writing for both British and American readers. At its best, distinctively American English is more direct and vivid than its British English equivalent. Many American words and expressions have passed into British English because they are shorter or more to the point: phrases like *lay off*, preferable to *make redundant*; *fire*, instead of *dismiss*. But American English also has a contrary tendency to lengthen words, creating a (to British readers) pompous tone: for instance, *transportation* (in British English, *transport*).

British English is slower than American English to accept new words and suspicious of short cuts, and sometimes it resists the use as verbs of nouns (*see* **grammar and syntax** in Part 1).

Below is a list of words that are acceptable in both American and British English, for use when you want to produce a single version of written material for both categories of reader:

ambience *not* ambiance
annex *not* annexe
among *not* amongst
artifact *not* artefact
backward *not* backwards
Bible (Scriptures), *not* bible
baptistry *not* baptistery
bus *not* coach
burned *not* burnt

canvases *not* canvasses
car rental *not* car hire
cater to *not* cater for *needs*
custom-made *not* bespoke
development *not* estate, *for housing*
diesel fuel *not* derv
disc *not* disk, *except in computing*

dispatch *not* despatch
encyclopedia *not* encyclopaedia
except for *not* save
farther *not* further, *for distance*
first name *not* Christian name
flip *not* toss, *for coin, etc*
focusing, focused, *etc*
fuel *not* petrol (UK) *or* gasoline (US)
forward *not* forwards
(eye)glasses *not* spectacles
gypsy *not* gipsy
hairdryer *not* hairdrier
horse-racing *not* just racing
insurance coverage *not* insurance cover
intermission *not* interval
jail *not* gaol
learned *not* learnt
line *not* queue
location *not* situation
maid *not* chambermaid
mathematics *not* maths (UK) *or* math (US)
motorcycle *not* motorbike
neat *not* spruce *or* tidy
newsstand *not* kiosk
nightgown *not* nightdress
orangeade/lemonade *not* orange/lemon squash
package *not* parcel
parking spaces/garage *not* car park (UK) *or* parking lot (US)
phoney *not* phony

refrigerator *not* fridge
railway station *not* railroad station
raincoat *not* mac, mackintosh
rent *not* hire, *except for people*
reservation, reserve *(seats, etc)* *not* booking, book
retired person *not* old-age pensioner (UK) *or* retiree (US)
slowdown *not* go-slow, *in production*
soccer *not* football, *except for American football*
spelled *not* spelt
spoiled *not* spoilt
street musician *not* busker
swap *not* swop
swimming *not* bathing
team *not* side, *in sport*
tearoom *not* teashop
thread *not* cotton
toilet *not* lavatory
toll-free *not* free of charge
tuna *not* tunny
underwear *not* pants *or* knickers; *or use lingerie for women's underwear*
unmistakable *not* unmistakeable
unspoiled *not* unspoilt
while *not* whilst
yogurt *not* yoghourt *or* yoghurt
zero *not* nought

The following lists draw attention to commonly used words and idioms that are spelt differently or have different meanings in American English and British English. When you do not want to produce a single version, follow one or other convention, and, if this means using a word that will mystify or mislead one group of readers, provide a translation. The lists do not cover slang or colloquialisms.

Accounting, banking and finance

British	American
acquisition accounting	purchase accounting
articles of association	bylaws
balance sheet	statement of financial position
banknote	bill
bonus or scrip issue	stock dividend or stock split
building society	savings and loan association
Chartered Accountant (CA)	Certified Public Accountant (CPA)
cheque (bank)	check
clerk (bank)	teller
closing rate method	current rate method
creditors	payables
current account	checking account
debtors	receivables
deferred tax	deferred income tax
depreciation	amortisation
exceptional items	unusual items
finance leases	capital leases
Inland Revenue	Internal Revenue
land and buildings	real estate
merger accounting	pooling of interests
nominal value	par value
non-pension post-employment benefits	OPEBS
old-age pension, state pension	Social Security
ordinary shares	common stock
own shares purchased but not cancelled	Treasury stock
pay rise	raise
preference shares	preferred stock
price rise	price hike
profit and loss account	income statement
profit for the financial year	net income
provisions	allowances
share premium	additional paid-in capital
shareholders' funds	stockholders' equity
stock	inventory
turnover	revenues
undistributable reserves	restricted surplus or deficiency

British	American
unit trust	mutual fund
value-added tax (VAT)	sales tax

Baby items

British	American
baby's dummy	pacifier
cot	crib
nappy	diaper
pram, push chair	baby carriage, stroller

Clothes

British	American
bag, handbag	purse, pocketbook
braces	suspenders
clothes cupboard/wardrobe	closet
dressing gown	bathrobe/housecoat/robe
jumper	sweater
ladder (in stocking)	run
pants	underpants
press studs	snaps
pyjamas	pajamas
tartan	plaid
trousers	pants, slacks, trousers
vest	undershirt
waistcoat	vest
zip (noun)	zipper

Food, cooking and eating

British	American
aubergine	eggplant
bill (restaurant)	check
biscuit (sweet)	cookie
biscuit (savoury)	cracker
black treacle	molasses
chilli/chillies	chile/chiles, chili powder, chili con carne
chips	French fries
cling film	plastic wrap
cooker	stove
cornflour	cornstarch
courgette	zucchini

British	American
crayfish	crawfish
crisps	potato chips
crystallised	candied
digestive biscuit	graham cracker
double cream	heavy cream
essence (eg, vanilla)	extract or flavoring
flour, plain	flour, all-purpose
flour, self-raising	flour, self-rising
flour, wholemeal	flour, whole-wheat
golden syrup	corn syrup
greengrocer's	vegetable store
grill (verb and noun)	broil (verb), broiler (noun)
icing sugar	powdered or confectioners' sugar
maize/sweetcorn	corn
minced meat	ground meat
pastry case	pie crust
pepper (red, green, etc)	sweet pepper, bell pepper, capsicum
pips	seeds (in fruit)
rocket (salad)	arugula
shortcrust pastry	short pastry/basic pie dough
single cream	light cream
soya	soy
spring onion	scallion, green onion
starter	appetizer
stoned (cherries, etc)	pitted
sultana	golden raisin
sweet shop	candy store
water biscuit	cracker

Homes and other buildings

British	American
camp bed	cot
cinema	movie theater
council estate	public housing
flat	apartment
ground floor	first floor
home from home	home away from home
homely	homey (homely = plain)
housing estate	housing development
lavatory, toilet	bathroom, restroom, washroom

British	American
lift	elevator
power point	electrical outlet, socket
property (land)	real estate
storey	story, floor
terraced house	row house

People, professions and politics

British	American
adopt a candidate	nominate a candidate
barrister	trial lawyer
doctor	physician
estate agent	realtor/real estate agent
ex-serviceman	veteran
headmistress/headmaster	principal
jeweller/jewellery	jeweler/jewelry
lawyer	attorney
manifesto (political)	platform
old-age pensioner, OAP	senior citizen, senior
sceptic	skeptic
senior (politician)	ranking
solicitor	attorney, lawyer
stand for office	run for office

Travel, transport and pedestrians

British	American
accelerator	gas pedal
bonnet, car	hood
boot, car	trunk
bumper	fender
car park	parking lot
caravan	trailer
coach	bus
crossroads/junction	intersection
cul-de-sac	dead end
demister	defogger
dual carriageway	four-lane (or divided) highway
estate car	station wagon
exhaust, car	muffler
flyover	overpass
gearbox	transmission
give way	yield

British	American
high street	main street
hire (a car)	rent or hire
indicator	turn signal
jump leads	jumper cables
lorry	truck
motor-racing	auto-racing
motorway	highway, freeway, expressway, throughway
number plate	licence plate
passenger	rider
pavement	sidewalk
pedestrian crossing	crosswalk
petrol	gasoline, gas
petrol station	gas/service station
puncture	flat tire
railway station	train station
rambler	hiker
return ticket	round-trip ticket
riding (horses)	horseback riding
ring road	beltway
rowing boat	rowboat
single ticket	one-way ticket
slip road	ramp
subway	pedestrian underpass
transport	transportation
turning (road)	turnoff
underground (or tube train)	subway
walk	hike (only if more energetic than a walk)
windscreen	windshield

Other words and phrases

British	American
aerial (TV)	antenna
anti-clockwise	counterclockwise
at weekends	on weekends
autumn	fall
bank holiday	public holiday
British Summer Time (BST)	Daylight Saving Time (DST)
chemist	drugstore, pharmacy

British	American
clever	smart
diary (appointments)	calendar
diary (record)	journal
dustbin	garbage can
earthed (wire)	ground
ex-serviceman, woman	veteran
film	movie
flannel	washcloth
from ... to ...	through
grey	gray
holiday	vacation
in (Fifth Avenue, etc)	on
lease of life	lease on life
mean (parsimonious)	stingy, tight (mean = nasty)
mobile phone	cell phone
oblige	obligate
ordinary	regular, normal
outside	outside of
over	overly
paddling pool	wading pool
plait	braid
post, post box	mail, mailbox
post code	zip code
postponement	rain-check
public school	private school
queue	line, line up
reverse charges	call collect
ring up, phone	call, phone
spanner	wrench
state school	public school
stupid	dumb
till	checkout
torch	flashlight
upmarket	upscale
work out (problem)	figure out
Zimmer frame	walker
zed (the letter z)	zee

part 3

useful reference

Abbreviations

Here is a list of some common business abbreviations.
    See also **abbreviations** in Part 1, **internet**, pages 190ff.

ABC	activity-based costing
ACH	automated clearing house
ADR	American depositary receipt
AG	Aktiengesellschaft (Austrian, German or Swiss public limited company)
AGM	annual general meeting
AIBD	Association of International Bond Dealers
AIDA	attention, interest, desire, action
AMEX	American Stock Exchange
APR	annualised percentage rate (of interest)
APT	arbitrage pricing theory
ARPU	average revenue per user/unit
ARR	accounting rate of return
ASB	Accounting Standards Board (UK)
ATM	automated teller machine
B2B	business-to-business
B2C	business-to-consumer
BACS	bankers' automated clearing services
BPO	business process outsourcing
BPR	business process re-engineering
BSI	British Standards Institution
CAPM	capital asset pricing model
CATS	certificate of accrual on Treasury securities; computer-assisted trading system
CCA	current cost accounting
CD	certificate of deposit
CEDEL	Centre de livraison de valeurs mobilières
CEO	chief executive officer
CFO	chief financial officer
CGT	capital gains tax

CHAPS	Clearing House Automated Payments Service
cif	cost, insurance, freight
CIO	chief information officer
COB	Commission des Opérations de Bourse (Stock Exchange Commission, France)
Consob	Commissione Nazionale per le Società e la Borsa (Stock Exchange Commission, Italy)
COO	chief operating officer
COLA	cost of living adjustment
COSA	cost of sales adjustment
CPA	certified public accountant (US); critical path analysis
CPP	current purchasing power (accounting)
CRC	current replacement cost
CRM	customer (or client) relationship management
CSR	corporate social responsibility
CTO	chief technology officer
CUPID	computer updated international database
CVP	cost-volume-profit analysis
DCF	discounted cash flow
EBIT	earnings before interest and tax
EBITDA	earnings before interest, tax, depreciation and amortisation
ECN	electronic communications network
EDP	electronic data processing
EFT	electronic funds transfer
EFTPOS	electronic funds transfer at point of sale
EMU	economic and monetary union
EPS	earnings per share
ERM	enterprise resource management
ESOP	employee stock or share ownership plan
ETF	exchange traded fund
EURIBOR	European Interbank Offered Rate
EV	economic value
EVA	economic value added
FAS	financial accounting standard (US)
FASB	Financial Accounting Standards Board (US)
FDI	foreign direct investment
Fed	Federal Reserve Board (US)
FIFO	first in, first out (used for valuing stock/inventory)
FMCG	fast-moving consumer goods
FMS	flexible manufacturing systems
fob	free on board

forex	foreign exchange
FRN	floating-rate note
FSA	Financial Services Authority (UK)
GAAP	generally accepted accounting principles (US)
GAAS	generally accepted audited standards
GDP	gross domestic product
GmbH	Gesellschaft mit beschränkter Haftung (Austrian, German or Swiss private limited company)
GNI	gross national income
GNP	gross national product
IAS	international accounting standard
IASB	International Accounting Standards Board
IASC	International Accounting Standards Committee
IBF	international banking facility
ICGN	International Corporate Governance Network
IFA	independent financial adviser
IFRS	International Financial Reporting Standards
ILO	International Labour Organisation
IPO	initial public offering
IRR	internal rate of return
IRS	Internal Revenue Service (US)
ISA	individual savings account
ISMA	International Securities Market Association
ISO	International Organisation for Standardisation
JIT	just-in-time
KISS	keep it simple stupid
LAN	local area network
LBO	leveraged buy-out
LIBOR	London Interbank Offered Rate
LIFO	last in, first out (used for valuing stock/inventory value, popular in US)
LNG	liquefied natural gas
LPG	liquefied petroleum gas
LSE	London Stock Exchange
M&A	mergers and acquisitions
MATIF	Marché à Terme des Instruments Financiers
MBI	management buy-in
MBO	management buy-out
MLR	minimum lending rate
NASDAQ	National Association of Securities Dealers Automated Quotations System (US)

NAV	net asset value
NBV	net book value
NGO	non-governmental organisation
NPV	net present value; no par value
NRV	net realisable value
Nymex	New York Mercantile Exchange
NYSE	New York Stock Exchange
OBU	offshore banking unit
ODM	original design manufacturer
OEIC	open-ended investment company
OTC	over the counter
P&L a/c	profit and loss account (income statement in the US)
PCAOB	Public Company Accounting Oversight Board
P/E	price/earnings (ratio)
PIN	personal identification number
PLC	public limited company (UK)
PPP	purchasing power parity
PSBR	public-sector borrowing requirement
R&D	research and development
RFID	radio frequency identification device
ROA	return on assets
ROCE	return on capital employed
ROE	return on equity
ROI	return on investment
RONA	return on net assets
ROOA	return on operating assets
ROTA	return on total assets
RPI	retail price index
RPIX	retail price index excluding mortgage interest payments
RTM	route to market
S&L	Savings and Loan Association (US)
SA	société anonyme (French, Belgian, Luxembourg or Swiss public limited company)
Sarl	société à responsabilité limitée (French, etc, private limited company)
SBU	strategic business unit
SCM	supply chain management
SDR	special drawing right (at the IMF)
SEAQ	Stock Exchange Automated Quotations (UK)
SEC	Securities and Exchange Commission (US)
SET	secure electronic transaction

SFO	Serious Fraud Office (UK)
SIB	Securities and Investments Board (UK)
SITC	standard international trade classification
SMART	specific, measurable, achievable, realistic, time bound
SME	small and medium-sized enterprises
SOHO	small office, home office
SOX	Sarbanes-Oxley Act (US)
SpA	societa per azioni (Italian public company)
SRO	self-regulating organisation
SSAP	Statement of Standard Accounting Practice (UK)
STRGL	statement of total recognised gains and losses
SWIFT	Society for Worldwide Interbank Financial Telecommunications
SWOT	strengths, weaknesses, opportunities, threats
T-bill	Treasury bill
TSR	total shareholder return
UCITS	Undertakings for Collective Investments in Transferable Securities
UEC	Union Européenne des Experts Comptables Economiques et Financiers
USM	unlisted securities market (UK)
USP	unique selling proposition
VAT	value-added tax
VCT	venture capital trust
WDV	written down value
WIIFM	what's in it for me
WIP	work-in-progress
XBRL	extensible business reporting language
ZBB	zero base budgeting

For international bodies and their abbreviations, *see* **organisations**, pages 214ff.

Beaufort Scale

For devotees of the shipping forecast, here is the World Meteorological Organisation's classification of wind forces and effects.

Conditions (abbreviated)				Equivalent speed at 10m height		
Force	Description	On land	At sea	knots	miles per hour	metres per second
0	Calm	Smoke rises vertically	Sea like a mirror	less than 1	less than 1	0.0–0.2
1	Light air	Smoke drifts	Ripples	1–3	1–3	0.3–1.5
2	Light breeze	Leaves rustle	Small wavelets	4–6	4–7	1.7–3.3
3	Gentle breeze	Wind extends light flag	Large wavelets, crests break	7–10	8–12	3.4–5.4
4	Moderate breeze	Raises paper and dust	Small waves, some white horses	11–16	13–18	5.5–7.9
5	Fresh breeze	Small trees in leaf sway	Moderate waves, many white horses	17–21	19–24	8.0–10.7
6	Strong breeze	Large branches in motion	Large waves form, some spray	22–27	25–31	10.8–13.8
7	Moderate gale or near gale	Whole trees in motion	Sea heaps up, white foam streaks	28–33	32–38	13.9–17.1
8	Fresh gale or gale	Breaks twigs off trees	Moderately high waves, well-marked foam streaks	34–40	39–46	17.2–20.7
9	Strong gale	Slight structural damage	High waves, crests start to tumble over	41–47	47–54	20.8–24.4
10	Whole gale or storm	Trees uprooted, considerable structural damage	Very high waves, white sea tumbles	48–55	55–63	24.5–28.4

Conditions (abbreviated)				Equivalent speed at 10m height		
Force	Description	On land	At sea	knots	miles per hour	metres per second
11	Storm or violent storm	Very rarely experienced, widespread damage	Exceptionally high waves, edges of wave crests blown to froth	56–63	64–72	28.5–32.6
12–17	Hurricane	Devastation with driving spray	Sea completely white	64–118	73–136	32.7–over

Business ratios

These are ratios commonly used in corporate financial analysis.

Working capital

Working capital ratio = current assets/current liabilities, where current assets = stock + debtors + cash at bank and in hand + quoted investments, etc, current liabilities = creditors + overdraft at bank + taxation + dividends, etc. The ratio varies according to type of trade and conditions; a ratio from 1 to 3 is usual, with a ratio above 2 taken to be safe.

Liquidity ratio = liquid ("quick") assets/current liabilities, where liquid assets = debtors + cash at bank and in hand + quoted investments (that is, assets which can be realised within a month or so, which may not apply to all investments); current liabilities are those which may need to be repaid within the same short period, which may not necessarily include a bank overdraft where it is likely to be renewed. The liquidity ratio is sometimes referred to as the "acid test"; a ratio under 1 suggests a possibly difficult situation, while too high a ratio may mean that assets are not being usefully employed.

Turnover of working capital = sales/average working capital. The ratio varies according to type of trade; generally a low ratio can mean poor use of resources, while too high a ratio can mean over-trading. Average working capital or average stock is found by taking the opening and closing working capital or stock and dividing by 2.

Turnover of stock = sales/average stock, or (where cost of sales is known) cost of sales/average stock. The cost of sales turnover figure is to be preferred as both figures are then on the same valuation basis. This ratio can be expressed as number of times per year, or time taken for stock to be turned over once = (52/number of times) weeks. A low turnover of stock can be a sign of stocks that are difficult to move, and usually indicates adverse conditions.

Turnover of debtors = sales/average debtors. This indicates efficiency in collecting accounts. An average credit period of about one month is usual, but varies according to credit stringency conditions in the economy.

Turnover of creditors = purchases/average creditors. Average payment period is best maintained in line with turnover of debtors.

Sales

Export ratio = exports as a percentage of sales.

Sales per employee = sales/average number of employees.

Assets

Ratios of assets can vary according to the measure of assets used:

Total assets = current assets + fixed assets + other assets, where fixed assets = property + plant and machinery + motor vehicles, etc, and other assets = long-term investment + goodwill, etc.

Net assets ("net worth") = total assets − total liabilities = share capital + reserves

Turnover of net assets = sales/average net assets. As for turnover of working capital, a low ratio can mean poor use of resources.

Assets per employee = assets/average number of employees. This indicates the amount of investment backing for employees.

Profits

Profit margin = (profit/sales) × 100 = profits as a percentage of sales; usually profits before tax.

Profitability = (profit/total assets) × 100 = profits as a percentage of total assets.

Return on capital = (profit/net assets) × 100 = profits as a percentage of net assets ("net worth" or "capital employed").

Profit per employee = profit/average number of employees.

Earnings per share (EPS) = after-tax profit − minorities/average number of shares in issue.

Calendars

There are five important solar calendars and the Jewish calendar, which is a combined solar/lunar calendar, like the Chinese.

Gregorian	Iranian[b]	Hindu[c]
January (31)[a]		
February (28 or 29)		
March (31)	Farvardin (31)	Caitra (30)
April (30)	Ordibehesht (31)	Vaisakha (31)
May (31)	Khordad (31)	Jyaistha (31)
June (30)	Tir (31)	Asadha (31)
July (31)	Mordad (31)	Sravana (31)
August (31)	Shahrivar (31)	Bhadrapada (31)
September (30)	Mehr (30)	Asvina (30)
October (31)	Aban (30)	Karttika (30)
November (30)	Azar (30)	Margasirsa (30)
December (31)	Dey (30)	Pausa (30)
January	Bahman (30)	Magha (30)
February	Esfand (28 or 29)	Phalguna (30)

Gregorian	Ethiopian[d]	Jewish[e]
September	Meskerem (30)	Tishri (30)
October	Tikemet (30)	Heshvan (29 or 30)
November	Hidar (30)	Kislev (29 or 30)
December	Tahesas (30)	Tebet (29)
January	Tir (30)	Shebat (30)
February	Yekatit (30)	Adar (29)
March	Megabit (30)	Nisan (30)
April	Miyaza (30)	Iyar (29)
May	Ginbot (30)	Sivan (30)
June	Sene (30)	Tammuz (29)
July	Hamle (30)	Ab (30)
August	Nehase (30+5 or 6)	Elul (29)
	Paguma	

a Figures in brackets denote the number of days in that month.

b Months begin about the 21st of the corresponding Gregorian month.

c Months begin about the 22nd of the corresponding Gregorian month.

d Months begin on the 11th of the corresponding Gregorian month. Ethiopia follows the Julian calendar.

e The date of the new year varies, but normally falls in the second half of September in the Gregorian calendar; the position is maintained by sometimes adding an extra period of 29 days, Adar Sheni, following the month of Adar.

Muslim calendar

Muslims use a lunar calendar which begins 10 or 11 days earlier each year in terms of the Gregorian. The months, whose names follow, do not have a fixed number of days. In each 30 years, 19 years have 354 days (are "common") and 11 have 355 days (are "intercalary").

Muharram	Rajab
Safar	Sha'ban
Rabi' I	Ramadan
Rabi' II	Shawwal
Jumada I	Dhu al-Qidah
Jumada II	Dhu al-Hijjah

The Muslim years in the columns below begin on the dates of the Gregorian calendar as shown.

1413	July 2nd 1992	1421	April 6th 2000
1414	June 21st 1993	1422	March 26th 2001
1415	June 9th 1994	1423	March 15th 2002
1416	May 31st 1995	1424	March 5th 2003
1417	May 19th 1996	1425	February 22nd 2004
1418	May 9th 1997	1426	February 10th 2005
1419	April 28th 1998	1427	January 31st 2006
1420	April 17th 1999	1428	January 20th 2007

Countries' administrative divisions

Here are the correct spellings of the main administrative subdivisions of the G10 group of industrial countries together with Russia. *See also* **countries and their inhabitants, placenames** in Part 1.

Belgium (Kingdom of Belgium)

Provinces

Antwerp	East Flanders
Brabant (Flemish, Walloon)	Hainaut

Liège
Limburg
Luxembourg

Namur
West Flanders

Canada

Provinces

Alberta
British Columbia
Manitoba
New Brunswick
Newfoundland

Nova Scotia
Ontario
Prince Edward Island
Quebec (Québec)
Saskatchewan

Territories

Northwest Territories
Nunavut

Yukon

France (Republic of France)

Regions

Alsace
Aquitaine
Auvergne
Basse-Normandie
Brittany (Bretagne)
Burgundy (Bourgogne)
Centre
Champagne-Ardenne
Corsica (Corse)
Franche-Comté
Haute-Normandie

Ile-de-France
Languedoc-Roussillon
Limousin
Lorraine
Midi-Pyrénées
Nord-Pas-de-Calais
Pays de la Loire
Picardy (Picardie)
Poitou-Charentes
Provence-Alpes-Côte d'Azur
Rhône-Alpes

Germany (Federal Republic of Germany)

States (in German *Länder*)

Baden-Württemberg

Bavaria (Bayern)

Berlin

Brandenburg
Bremen
Hamburg
Hesse (Hessen)
Lower Saxony (Niedersachsen)

Mecklenburg-West Pomerania
    (Vorpommern)
North Rhine-Westphalia
    (Nordrhein-Westfalen)
Rhineland-Palatinate (Rheinland-
    Pfalz)
Saarland
Saxony (Sachsen)
Saxony-Anhalt (Sachsen-Anhalt)
Schleswig-Holstein
Thuringia (Thüringen)

Italy (Italian Republic)

Regions

Abruzzo	Marches (Marche)
Apulia (Puglia)	Molise
Basilicata	Piedmont (Piemonte)
Calabria	Sardinia (Sardegna)
Campania	Sicily (Sicilia)
Emilia-Romagna	Tuscany (Toscana)
Friuli-Venezia Giulia	Trentino-Alto Adige
Lazio	Umbria
Liguria	Valle d'Aosta
Lombardy (Lombardia)	Veneto

Japan

Japan is divided into regions (in bold italics), which are divided into prefectures.

Hokkaido
Hokkaido

Tohoku

Aomori	Miyagi	Yamagata
Iwate	Akita	Fukushima

Kanto

Ibaraki	Saitama	Tokyo
Tochigi	Chiba	Kanagawa
Gumma		

Chubu

Niigata	Fukui	Gifu
Toyama	Yamanashi	Shizuoka
Ishikawa	Nagano	Aichi

Kinki

Mie	Osaka	Nara
Shiga	Hyogo	Wakayama
Kyoto		

Chugoku

Tottori	Yamaguchi	Kagawa
Shimane	Shikoku	Ehime
Okayama	Tokushima	Kochi
Hiroshima		

Kyushu

Fukuoka	Kumamoto	Kagoshima
Saga	Oita	Okinawa
Nagasaki	Miyazaki	

Netherlands (Kingdom of the Netherlands)

Provinces

Drenthe	Noord-Brabant
Flevoland	Noord-Holland
Friesland	Overijssel
Gelderland	Utrecht
Groningen	Zeeland
Limburg	Zuid-Holland

Russia (Russian Federation)

There are 89 members (federal territorial units) of the Russian Federation, consisting of 21 republics, six *krais* (provinces), 49 *oblasts* (regions), two cities of federal status (Moscow and St Petersburg), one autonomous *oblast* (the Jewish Autonomous Area) and ten *okrugs* (districts), under the jurisdiction of the *oblast* or *krai* within which they are situated. Each unit is grouped into one of seven federal districts.

Federal districts

Central	South
Far East	Urals
North-West	Volga
Siberian	

Republics

Adygeya	Kareliya
Bashkortostan	Khakasiya
Buryatiya	Komi
Chechnya[a]	Marii-El
Chuvashiya	Mordoviya
Dagestan	North Osetiya-Alaniya
Gorno-Altai	Sakha (Yakutiya)
Ingushetiya	Tatarstan
Kabardino-Balkariya	Tyva
Kalmykiya	Udmurtiya
Karachayevo-Cherkessiya	

a   Governed federally.

Krais

Altai	Krasnoyarsk
Khabarovsk	Primorskii
Krasnodar	Stavropol

Autonomous okrugs

Agin-Buryat	Koryak
Chukotka	Nenets
Evenk	Taimyr
Khanty-Mansi	Ust-Orda Buryat
Komi-Permyak	Yamal-Nenets

Sweden

Sweden is traditionally divided into three major regions, which are further subdivided into 25 provinces (*landskap*) which have no administrative function.

Gotaland

Blekinge	Halland	Skane
Bohuslan	Oland	Smaland
Dalsland	Ostergötland	Vastergötland
Gotland		

Norrland

Angermanland	Harjedalen	Medelpad
Gastrikland	Jamtland	Norrbotten
Halsingland	Lappland	Vasterbotten

Svealand

Dalarna (southern parts)	Södermanland	Varmland
Naärke	Uppland	Vastmanland

Administrative divisions (lan)

Blekinge	Kalmar	Stockholm
Dalarna	Kronoberg	Uppsala
Garleborg	Norrbotten	Varmland
Gotaland	Orebro	Vasterbotten
Gotland	Ostergotland	Vasternorrland
Halland	Skane	Vastmanland
Jamtland	Sodermanland	Vastra
Jonkoping		

Switzerland

Also known as Confoederatio Helvetica, hence the abbreviation CH.

"Confoederatio" means "confederation", "Helvetica" derives from the Latin word "Helvetia", for the area which later became Switzerland. It consists of 23 cantons, as follows, in their official order.

Zurich

Bern

Luzern (Lucerne)

Uri

Schwyz

Unterwalden
  (Obwalden/Nidwalden)

Glarus

Zug

Freiburg/Fribourg

Solothurn

Basel

Schaffhausen

Appenzell (Appenzell Ausserrhoden/
  Appenzell Innerrhoden)

Sankt Gallen

Graubünden

Aargau

Thurgau

Ticino

Vaud

Valais

Neuchâtel

Geneva

Jura

United Kingdom

England Unitary Authorities

Barnsley

Bath and North-east Somerset

Birmingham

Blackburn with Darwen

Blackpool

Bolton

Bournemouth

Bracknell Forest

Bradford

Brighton and Hove

Bristol

Bury

Calderdale

Coventry

Darlington

Derby

Doncaster

Dudley

East Riding of Yorkshire

Gateshead

Halton

Hartlepool

Herefordshire

Isle of Wight

Kingston upon Hull

Kirklees

Knowsley

Leeds

Leicester

Liverpool

Luton

Manchester

Medway

Middlesbrough

Milton Keynes

Newcastle upon Tyne

North-east Lincolnshire

North Lincolnshire

North Somerset

North Tyneside

Nottingham

Oldham

Peterborough
Plymouth
Poole
Portsmouth
Reading
Redcar and Cleveland
Rochdale
Rotherham
Rutland
St Helens
Salford
Sandwell
Sefton
Sheffield
Slough
Solihull
South Gloucestershire
Southampton
Southend
South Tyneside

Stockport
Stockton-on-Tees
Stoke-on-Trent
Sunderland
Swindon
Tameside
Telford and Wrekin
Thurrock
Torbay
Trafford
Wakefield
Walsall
Warrington
West Berkshire
Wigan
Windsor and Maidenhead
Wirral
Wokingham
Wolverhampton
York

England Non-Metropolitan Counties

Bedfordshire
Buckinghamshire
Cambridgeshire
Cheshire
Cornwall/Isles of Scilly
Cumbria
Derbyshire
Devon
Dorset
Durham
East Sussex
Essex
Gloucestershire
Hampshire
Hertfordshire
Kent
Lancashire

Leicestershire
Lincolnshire
Norfolk
Northamptonshire
Northumberland
North Yorkshire
Nottinghamshire
Oxfordshire
Shropshire
Somerset
Staffordshire
Suffolk
Surrey
Warwickshire
West Sussex
Wiltshire
Worcestershire

Wales *Unitary Authorities*

Blaenau Gwent
Bridgend
Caerphilly
Cardiff
Carmarthenshire
Ceredigion
Conwy
Denbighshire
Flintshire
Gwynedd
Isle of Anglesey

Merthyr Tydfil
Monmouthshire
Neath Port Talbot
Newport
Pembrokeshire
Powys
Rhondda, Cynon, Taff
Swansea
Torfaen
Vale of Glamorgan
Wrexham

Scotland *Unitary Authorities*

Aberdeen City
Aberdeenshire
Angus
Argyll and Bute
Clackmannanshire
Dumfries and Galloway
Dundee City
East Ayrshire
East Dunbartonshire
East Lothian
East Renfrewshire
Edinburgh, City of
Eilean Siar/Western Isles
Falkirk
Fife
Glasgow City

Highland
Inverclyde
Midlothian
Moray
North Ayrshire
North Lanarkshire
Orkney Islands
Perth and Kinross
Renfrewshire
Scottish Borders
Shetland Islands
South Ayrshire
South Lanarkshire
Stirling
West Dunbartonshire
West Lothian

Northern Ireland *Councils*

Antrim
Ards
Armagh
Ballymena
Ballymoney
Banbridge
Belfast
Carrickfergus
Castlereagh
Coleraine
Cookstown

Craigavon
Down
Dungannon
Fermanagh
Larne
Limavady
Lisburn
Londonderry/Derry
Magherafelt
Moyle
Newry and Mourne

Newtownabbey
North Down

Omagh
Strabane

Northern Ireland *Counties*
Antrim
Armagh
Belfast City
Down

Fermanagh
Londonderry/Derry
Londonderry City
Tyrone

United States
States
Alabama (AL)
Alaska (AK)
Arizona (AZ)
Arkansas (AR)
California (CA)
Colorado (CO)
Connecticut (CT)
Delaware (DE)
Federal District of Columbia (DC)[a]
Florida (FL)
Georgia (GA)
Hawaii (HI)
Idaho (ID)
Illinois (IL)
Indiana (IN)
Iowa (IA)
Kansas (KS)
Kentucky (KY)
Louisiana (LA)
Maine (MA)
Maryland (MD)
Massachusetts (MA)
Michigan (MI)
Minnesota (MN)
Mississippi (MS)
Missouri (MO)

Montana (MT)
Nebraska (NE)
Nevada (NV)
New Hampshire (NH)
New Jersey (NJ)
New Mexico (NM)
New York (NY)
North Carolina (NC)
North Dakota (ND)
Ohio (OH)
Oklahoma (OK)
Oregon (OR)
Pennsylvania (PA)
Puerto Rico (PR)
Rhode Island (RI)
South Carolina (SC)
South Dakota (SD)
Tennessee (TN)
Texas (TX)
Utah (UT)
Vermont (VT)
Virginia (VA)
Washington (WA)
West Virginia (WV)
Wisconsin (WI)
Wyoming (WY)

a DC is not a state.

Currencies

See also **currencies** in Part 1 for *The Economist* newspaper usage.

Country	Currency	Symbol
Afghanistan	afghani	Af
Albania	lek	Lk
Algeria	Algerian dinar	AD
Angola	kwanza	Kz
Argentina	peso	Ps
Armenia	dram	Dram
Aruba	Aruban florin	Afl
Australia	Australian dollar	A$
Austria	euro	€
Azerbaijan	manat	Manat
Bahamas	Bahamian dollar	B$
Bahrain	Bahraini dinar	BD
Bangladesh	taka	Tk
Barbados	Barbadian dollar	Bd$
Belarus	rubel	BRb
Belgium	euro	€
Belize	Belize dollar	Bz$
Benin	CFA franc	CFAfr[a]
Bermuda	Bermuda dollar	Bda$
Bhutan	ngultrum	Nu
Bolivia	boliviano	Bs
Bosnia & Hercegovina	convertible marka	KM
Botswana	pula	P
Brazil	*real* (pl. *reais*)	R
Brunei	Brunei dollar/ringgit	Br$
Bulgaria	lev	Lv
Burkina Faso	CFA franc	CFAfr
Burundi	Burundi franc	Bufr
Cambodia	riel	CR
Cameroon	CFA franc	CFAfr
Canada	Canadian dollar	C$
Cape Verde	Cape Verde escudo	CVEsc
Central African Republic	CFA franc	CFAfr
Chad	CFA franc	CFAfr
Chile	Chilean peso	Ps
China	yuan/renminbi	Rmb
Colombia	Colombian peso	Ps

Country	Currency	Symbol
Comoros	Comorian franc	Cfr
Congo (Brazzaville)	CFA franc	CFAfr
Congo (Dem. Rep. of)	Congolese franc	FCNZ
Costa Rica	Costa Rican colón	C
Côte d'Ivoire	CFA franc	CFAfr
Croatia	kuna	HRK
Cuba	Cuban peso	Ps
Cyprus	Cyprus pound/Turkish lira	C£/TL
Czech Republic	koruna	Kc
Denmark	Danish krone	DKr
Djibouti	Djibouti franc	Dfr
Dominican Republic	Dominican Republic peso	Ps
Dubai	UAE dirham	Dh
East Timor	US dollar	US$
Ecuador	US dollar	US$
Egypt	Egyptian pound	£E
El Salvador	El Salvador colón	C
Equatorial Guinea	CFA franc	CFAfr
Eritrea	nafka	Nfa
Estonia	kroon	EEK
Ethiopia	birr	Birr
Fiji	Fiji or Fijian dollar	F$
Finland	euro	€
France	euro	€
Gabon	CFA franc	CFAfr
The Gambia	dalasi	D
Georgia	lari	Lari
Germany	euro	€
Ghana	cedi	C
Greece	euro	€
Grenada	East Caribbean dollar	EC$
Guatemala	quetzal	Q
Guinea	Guinean franc	Gnf
Guinea-Bissau	CFA franc	CFAfr
Guyana	Guyanese dollar	G$
Haiti	gourde	G
Honduras	lempira	La
Hong Kong	Hong Kong dollar	HK$
Hungary	forint	Ft
Iceland	krona	Ikr

Country	Currency	Symbol
India	Indian rupee	Rs
Indonesia	rupiah	Rp
Iran	rial	IR
Iraq	New Iraqi dinar	NID
Ireland	euro	€
Israel	New Israeli shekel	NIS
Italy	euro	€
Jamaica	Jamaican dollar	J$
Japan	yen	¥
Jordan	Jordanian dinar	JD
Kazakhstan	tenge	Tenge
Kenya	Kenya shilling	KSh
Kirgizstan	som	Som
North Korea	won or North Korean won	Won
South Korea	won or South Korean won	W
Kuwait	Kuwaiti dinar	KD
Laos	kip	K
Latvia	lat	LVL
Lebanon	Lebanese pound	L£
Lesotho	loti (pl. maloti)	M
Liberia	Liberian dollar	L$
Libya	Libyan dinar	LD
Lithuania	litas	LTL
Luxembourg	euro	€
Macau	pataca	MPtc
Macedonia	denar	Den
Malagasy	Malagasy franc	Mgfr
Malawi	kwacha	MK
Malaysia	Malaysian dollar/ringgit	M$
Mali	CFA franc	CFAfr
Malta	Maltese lira	Lm
Mauritania	ouguiya	UM
Mauritius	Mauritius rupee	MRs
Mexico	Mexican peso	Ps
Moldova	Moldavian leu (pl. lei)	Lei
Mongolia	togrog	Tg
Montenegro	euro	€
Morocco	dirham	Dh
Mozambique	metical	MT
Myanmar	kyat	Kt

Country	Currency	Symbol
Namibia	Namibia dollar	N$
Nepal	Nepalese rupee	NRs
Netherlands	euro	€
Netherlands Antilles	Netherlands Antilles florin	NAf
New Caledonia	French Pacific franc	CFPfr
New Zealand	New Zealand dollar	NZ$
Nicaragua	córdoba	C
Niger	CFA franc	CFAfr
Nigeria	naira	N
Norway	Norwegian krone	NKr
Oman	Omani rial	OR
Pakistan	Pakistan or Pakistani rupee	PRs
Palestinian Territories	Jordanian dinar, New Israeli shekel	JD, NIS
Panama	balboa	B
Papua New Guinea	kina	Kina
Paraguay	guarani	G
Peru	nuevo sol	Ns
Philippines	Philippine peso	P
Poland	zloty	Z
Portugal	euro	€
Puerto Rico	US dollar	US$
Qatar	Qatari riyal	QR
Romania	leu (pl. lei)	Lei
Russia	rouble	Rb
Rwanda	Rwandan franc	Rwfr
Samoa	tala or Samoan dollar	Tala
São Tomé & Príncipe	dobra	Db
Saudi Arabia	Saudi riyal	SR
Senegal	CFA franc	CFAfr
Serbia and Montenegro	dinar	YuD
Seychelles	Seychelles rupee	SRs
Sierra Leone	leone	Le
Singapore	Singapore dollar	S$
Slovakia	koruna	Sk
Slovenia	tolar	SIT
Solomon Islands	Solomon Islands dollar	SI$
Somalia	Somali shilling	SoSh
South Africa	rand	R
Spain	euro	€
Sri Lanka	Sri Lanka or Sri Lankan rupee	SLRs

Country	Currency	Symbol
Sudan	Sudanese dinar	SD
Suriname	Suriname guilder	SG
Swaziland	lilangeni (pl. emalangeni)	E
Sweden	Swedish krona	SKr
Switzerland	Swiss franc	Swfr
Syria	Syrian pound	S£
Taiwan	New Taiwan dollar	NT$
Tajikistan	somoni	S
Tanzania	Tanzanian shilling	TSh
Thailand	baht	Bt
Togo	CFA franc	CFAfr
Tonga	pa'anga or tonga/tongan dollar	T$
Trinidad & Tobago	TT dollar	TT$
Tunisia	Tunisian dinar	TD
Turkey	Turkish lira	TL
Turkmenistan	manat	Manat
Turks and Caicos Islands	dollar	US$
Uganda	New Ugandan shilling	NUSh
Ukraine	hryvnya	HRN
United Arab Emirates	UAE dirham	Dh
United Kingdom	pound/sterling	£
United States	dollar	$
Uruguay	Uruguayan new peso	Ps
Uzbekistan	som	Som
Vanuatu	vatu	Vt
Venezuela	bolívar	Bs
Vietnam	dong	D
Western Samoa	tala	Tala
Windward & Leeward Islands[b]	East Caribbean dollar	EC$
Yemen	Yemeni rial	YR
Zambia	kwacha	ZK
Zimbabwe	Zimbabwe dollar	Z$

a CFA = Communauté financière africaine in West African area and Coopération financière en Afrique centrale in Central African area. Used in monetary areas of West and Central Africa. 1 franc CFA = 1 French centime.
b Antigua and Barbuda, Dominica, Grenada, Monserrat, St Kitts-Nevis, St Lucia, St Vincent & Grenadines, the British Virgin Islands.

Earthquakes

An earthquake is measured in terms of its magnitude.

Magnitude	Joules	Explosion equivalent TNT terms	Nuclear terms
0[a]	7.9×10^2	175mg	
1	6.0×10^4	13g	
2	4.0×10^6	0.89kg	
3	2.4×10^8	53kg	
4	1.3×10^{10}	3 tons	
5[b]	6.3×10^{11}	140 tons	
6[c]	2.7×10^{13}	6 kilotons	$^1/_3$ atomic bomb
7	1.1×10^{15}	240 kilotons	12 atomic bombs
8	3.7×10^{16}	8.25 megatons	$^1/_3$ hydrogen bomb
9	1.1×10^{18}	250 megatons	13 hydrogen bombs
10	3.2×10^{19}	7,000 megatons	350 hydrogen bombs

a About equal to the shock caused by an average man jumping from a table.
b Potentially damaging to structures.
c Potentially capable of general destruction; widespread damage is usually caused above magnitude 6.5.

Here are some examples.

	Magnitude		Magnitude
Banda Sea, Indonesia, 1938	8.5	Northern Sumatra, 2005	8.7
Chile, 1906	8.5	Ecuador, 1906	8.8
Kamchatka, 1923	8.5	Kamchatka, 1952	9.0
Kuril Islands, 1963	8.5	Northern Sumatra, 2004 (called the tsunami)	9.0
Ningxia-Gansu, China, 1920	8.6	Andreanof Islands, Alaska, 1957	9.1
Sanriku, Japan, 1933	8.6	Prince William Sound, Alaska, 1964	9.2
India/Assam/Tibet, 1950	8.7	Chile, 1960	9.5
Rat Islands, Alaska, 1965	8.7	Krakatoa, 1883 (estimate)	9.9

Elements

These are the natural and artificially created chemical elements.

Name	Symbol	Name	Symbol
Actinium	Ac	Hassium	Hs
Aluminium	Al	Helium	He
Americium	Am	Holmium	Ho
Antimony (Stibium)	Sb	Hydrogen	H
Argon	Ar	Indium	In
Arsenic	As	Iodine	I
Astatine	At	Iridium	Ir
Barium	Ba	Iron (Ferrum)	Fe
Berkelium	Bk	Krypton	Kr
Beryllium	Be	Lanthanum	La
Bismuth	Bi	Lawrencium	Lw
Bohrium	Bh	Lead (Plumbum)	Pb
Boron	B	Lithium	Li
Bromine	Br	Lutetium	Lu
Cadmium	Cd	Magnesium	Mg
Caesium	Cs	Manganese	Mn
Calcium	Ca	Meitnerium	Mt
Californium	Cf	Mendelevium	Md
Carbon	C	Mercury (Hydrargyrum)	Hg
Cerium	Ce	Molybdenum	Mo
Chlorine	Cl	Neodymium	Nd
Chromium	Cr	Neon	Ne
Cobalt	Co	Neptunium	Np
Copper (Cuprum)	Cu	Nickel	Ni
Curium	Cm	Niobium (Columbium)	Nb
Dubnium	Db	Nitrogen	N
Dysprosium	Dy	Nobelium	No
Einsteinium	Es	Osmium	Os
Erbium	Er	Oxygen	O
Europium	Eu	Palladium	Pd
Fermium	Fm	Phosphorus	P
Fluorine	F	Platinum	Pt
Francium	Fr	Plutonium	Pu
Gadolinium	Gd	Polonium	Po
Gallium	Ga	Potassium (Kalium)	K
Germanium	Ge	Praseodymium	Pr
Gold (Aurum)	Au	Promethium	Pm
Hafnium	Hf	Protactinium	Pa

Name	Symbol	Name	Symbol
Radium	Ra	Tellurium	Te
Radon	Rn	Terbium	Tb
Rhenium	Re	Thallium	Tl
Rhodium	Rh	Thorium	Th
Rubidium	Rb	Thulium	Tm
Ruthenium	Ru	Tin (Stannum)	Sn
Rutherfordium	Rf	Titanium	Ti
Samarium	Sm	Tungsten (Wolfram)	W
Scandium	Sc	Ununbium	Uub
Seaborgium	Sg	Ununnilium	Uun
Selenium	Se	Unununium	Uuu
Silicon	Si	Uranium	U
Silver (Argentum)	Ag	Vanadium	V
Sodium (Natrium)	Na	Xenon	Xe
Strontium	Sr	Ytterbium	Yb
Sulphur	S	Yttrium	Y
Tantalum	Ta	Zinc	Zn
Technetium	Tc	Zirconium	Zr

Footnotes, sources, references

Footnotes appear at the foot of the page (or column) on which they occur; endnotes are listed at the end of a chapter or in one batch at the end of the work. The method depends on the publisher's conventions, the type of work and the readership. The author may have little say in the matter. Footnotes may also contain additional snippets of material or comment that the author feels is not appropriate to the main text.

1   Charts, tables and figures: place source underneath.
2   Page numbers: "page" is usually abbreviated to p., plural pp., except, for example, in *The Economist*, where they are written in full.
3   Footnote numbers, which are conventionally superscript, go after the punctuation in English works, before in American. If there are not many footnotes, some publishers prefer to use asterisks, daggers, etc.

The main methods (other than *The Economist*'s) of referring to sources are: the author-date (Harvard) system; the author-number (Vancouver) system; and the author-title system.

The Economist Books should be in quotation marks, periodicals in italics, authors, publishers, addresses (optional) and prices in roman. Commas should follow the title and the publisher (if an address is given). The other elements should each be followed by a full stop.

> "A Child's Guide to the Dismal Science", by Rupert Penandwig. Haphazard House, 1234 Madison Avenue, New York, NY 10019. $28.

In charts and tables, no final stop is necessary.

Harvard system The most commonly used system in physical and social sciences publications. The author's name and year of publication appear in parentheses in the text with the full details at the end of the publication in a list of references. For example:

> The variety of wildlife in our gardens (Murphy 2003) is amazing ...
> In his research, Murphy (2003) finds that ...

If you wish to include the page numbers, write Murphy 2003: 165 or Murphy 2003, p. 165 or pp. 165–6.

The reference section contains the full details:

> Murphy, P.L. (2003), *Birds, Bees and Butterflies* (Garden Press, London).

Vancouver system Most commonly used in scientific journals. Each publication is numbered and the text reference is a superscript number. For example:

> The variety of wildlife in our gardens[15] is amazing ...

The reference section contains the full details:

> 15. Murphy, P.L., *Birds, Bees and Butterflies* (London: Garden Press, 2003).

Note that any addition or subtraction from the list means that all subsequent items and the references will have to be renumbered.

author-title system Also known as the short-title system. A full reference is given only on the first mention in the chapter (or book if there is a bibliography).

This is mostly for academic works. The whole title is cited in the first footnote, for example P.H. Clarke, *Visions of Utopia*, at which point you put, "hereafter Clarke, *Utopia*". Then on subsequent references you simply write "Clarke, *Utopia*", with page numbers if you wish.

mixed system Another system is quite common in academic publications. A superscript number is placed in the text which refers to the number of the footnote (or endnote) which may be numbered per chapter or per book and is found at the foot of the page, the end of the chapter or the end of the book. The footnote consists of the bibliographical reference in full if there is no reference section at the end or abbreviated if there is.

Notes

- ibid. (abbreviation of *ibidem*, in the same place), not italic, is used to mean that the quote comes from the same source.
- op. cit. (abbreviation of *opere citato*, in the work quoted), not italic, is used to mean that the source has already been given.

Fractions

Do not mingle fractions with decimals. If you need to convert one to the other, use this table. *See also* **figures** in Part 1.

Fraction	Decimal equivalent
1/2	0.5
1/3	0.333
1/4	0.25
1/5	0.2
1/6	0.167
1/7	0.143
1/8	0.125
1/9	0.111
1/10	0.1
1/11	0.091
1/12	0.083
1/13	0.077
1/14	0.071
1/15	0.067
1/16	0.063
1/17	0.059
1/18	0.056
1/19	0.053
1/20	0.05

Geological eras

Astronomers and geologists give this broad outline of the ages of the universe and the earth.

Era, period and epoch		Years ago (m)	Characteristics
Origin of the universe (estimates vary markedly)		20,000– 10,000	
Origin of the sun		5,000	
Origin of the earth		4,600	
Pre-Cambrian			
Archean		4,000	First signs of fossilised microbes
Proterozoic		2,500	
Palaeozoic			
Cambrian		570	First appearance of abundant fossils
Ordovician (obsolete)		500	Vertebrates emerge
Silurian		440	Fishes emerge
Devonian		400	Primitive plants emerge
Carboniferous		350	Amphibians emerge
Permian		270	Reptiles emerge
Mesozoic			
Triassic		250	Seed plants emerge
Jurassic		210	Age of dinosaurs
Cretaceous		145	Flowering plants emerge; dinosaurs extinct at end of this period
Cenozoic			
Palaeocene		65	
Tertiary:	Eocene	55	Mammals emerge
	Oligocene	40	
	Miocene	25	
	Pliocene	5	
Quaternary:	Pleistocene	2	Ice ages; stone age man emerges
	Holocene or Recent	c. 10,000[a]	Modern man emerges

a 10,000 years, not 10,000m years.

Internet

Here is a list of abbreviations used in connection with the internet.

ADSL	asynchronous digital subscriber line
AOL	America Online
ASCII	American standard code for information interchange
ASP	application service provider
BCC	blind carbon copy
BPS	bits per second
CAD	computer aided design
CC	carbon copy
CDMA	code-division multiple access
CSS	cascading style sheet
CGI	common gateway interface
COM	component object model
CORBA	common object request broker architecture
DCOM	distributed component object model
DES	data encryption standard
DHCP	dynamic host configuration protocol
DHTML	dynamic hypertext mark-up language
DOM	document object model
DNS	domain name system
DSL	digital subscriber line (or loop)
EDI	electronic data interchange
EFF	electronic frontier foundation
FAQ	frequently asked questions
FDM	frequency-division multiplexing
FSF	free software foundation
FTP	file transfer protocol
GIF	graphics interchange format
GPRS	general packet radio service
GSM	global system for mobile communications
GUI	graphical user interface
HTML	hypertext mark-up language
HTTP	hypertext transfer protocol

IAB	internet architecture board
IANA	internet assigned names authority
ICANN	internet corporation for assigned names and numbers
ICQ	I seek you
IDS	intrusion-detection system
IETF	internet engineering task force
IM	instant messaging
IMAP	internet message access protocol
IP	internet protocol
IPTV	internet protocol television
IRC	internet relay chat
IRL	in real life
ISDN	integrated services digital network
ISP	internet service provider
JANET	joint academic network
JPEG	joint picture experts group (or **JPG**)
KBPS	kilobits per second
LAN	local area network
LDAP	lightweight directory access protocol
LINX	London internet exchange
MBPS	millions of bits per second
MIME	multipurpose internet mail extensions
MMS	multimedia message service
MOO	MUD Object Oriented (MUD stands for multi-user dungeon)
MSN	Microsoft network
MPEG	motion picture experts group
NAP	network access point
NCSA	National Centre for Supercomputing Applications
NNTP	network news transport protocol
OFDM	orthogonal frequency-division multiplexing
OSI	open source initiative
PCS	personal communications service
PDA	personal digital assistant
PDF	portable document format
PGP	pretty good privacy
PHP	hypertext preprocessor
PKI	public key infrastructure
POP	point of presence
POP3	post office protocol (latest version)
POTS	plain old telephone service
PPP	point-to-point protocol
QOS	quality of service

RDF	resource description framework
RFC	request for comments
RSS	really simple syndication or rich site summary
SMS	short message service
SMTP	simple mail transport protocol
SOAP	simple access object protocol
SQL	structured query language
SSL	secure sockets layer
TCP	transmission control protocol
TCP/IP	transmission control protocol/internet protocol
TDM	time-division multiplexing
TLA	three-letter acronym
TLD	top-level domain
TTP	trusted third party
UDDI	universal description, discovery and integration
UDRP	uniform dispute resolution policy
UMTS	universal mobile telecommunications system
URI	uniform resource identifier
URL	uniform resource locator
UUCP	unix-to-unix copy protocol
UWB	ultra-wideband
VBNS	very high speed backbone network service
VISP	virtual internet service provider
VM	virtual machine
VOIP	voice over IP
VPN	virtual private network
VRML	virtual reality modelling language
W3C	world wide web consortium
WAP	wireless application protocol
WASP	wireless application service provider
W-CDMA	wideband code-division multiple access
WDM	wavelength-division multiplexing
WEP	wired equivalent privacy
WI-FI	wireless fidelity
WIMAX	worldwide interoperability for microwave access
WMA	windows media audio
WML	wireless mark-up language
WSDL	web services description language
WWW	world wide web
XHTML	extensible hypertext mark-up language
XML	extensible mark-up language
XSL	extensible stylesheet language

Latin

Here are some common Latin words and phrases, together with their translations.

ab initio	from the beginning
ad hoc	for this object or purpose (implied and "this one only"); therefore, without a system, spontaneously
ad hominem	to an individual's interests or passions; used of an argument that takes advantage of the character of the person on the other side
ad infinitum	to infinity, that is, endlessly
ad lib., ad libitum	at pleasure. Used adverbially or even as a verb when it means to invent or extemporise
ad nauseam	to a sickening extent
ad valorem	according to value (as opposed to volume)
a fortiori	with stronger reason
annus mirabilis	wonderful year, used to describe a special year, one in which more than one memorable thing has happened; for instance 1666, the year of the Great Fire of London and the English defeats of the Dutch
a priori	from cause to effect, that is, deductively or from prior principle
casus belli	the cause of war
carpe diem	literally pluck the day, but seize the day is more common; enjoy the moment; make the most of life
cave!	"Watch out!" (imperative); once used at boys' private schools in Britain
caveat emptor	let the buyer beware
ceteris paribus	other things being equal
cf	short for confer, meaning compare
circa	around or about: used for dates and large quantities; can be abbreviated to c or c.
de facto	in point of fact
de jure	from the law; by right

de minimis   abbreviation of *de minimis non curat lex*, meaning
                        the law is not concerned with trivial matters; too
                        small to be taken seriously

de profundis   from the depths

deus ex machina   God from a machine; first used of a Greek
                        theatrical convention, where a god would swing
                        on to the stage, high up in a machine, solving
                        humanly insoluble problems and thus resolving
                        the action of a play. Now used to describe a
                        wholly outside person who puts matters right

eg, exempli gratia for example

et al., et alii   and others, used as an abbreviation in
                        bibliographies when citing multiple editorship
                        or authorship to save the writer the bother of
                        writing out all the names. Thus, A. Bloggs *et al.*,
                        *The Occurrence of Endangered Species in the Genus
                        Orthodoptera*

ex ante   before the event

ex cathedra   from the chair of office, authoritatively

ex officio   by virtue of one's office, not unofficially

ex gratia   as a favour, not under any compulsion

ex parte   from or for one side only

ex post facto, ex   after the fact, retrospectively
  post

ex tempore   off the cuff, without preparation (extempore)

habeas corpus   that you have a body; a writ to bring a person
                        before a court, in most cases to ensure that the
                        person's imprisonment is not illegal

horror vacui   literally, "fear of empty space"; the compulsion
                        to make marks in every space. *Horror vacui* is
                        indicated by a crowded design

ibid., ibidem   in the same place; used in footnotes in academic
                        works to mean that the quote comes from the
                        same source

idem   the same, as mentioned before; like ibidem

ie, id est   that is, explains the material immediately in front
                        of it

in absentia   in the absence of, used as "absent"

in camera   in a (private) room, that is, not in public

in flagrante delicto in the act of committing a crime; caught red-
                        handed; an expression that seems to have
                        developed a sexual connotation

in loco	in the place of; eg, in loco parentis, in the place of a parent
in re	in the matter of
in situ	in (its) original place
inter alia/inter alios	among other things or people
intra vires	within the permitted powers (contrast with ultra vires)
ipso facto	by that very fact, in the fact itself
lapsus linguae	a slip of the tongue
lingua franca	a common tongue
loc. cit., loco citato	in the place cited; used in footnotes to mean that the source of the reference or quote has already been given
mea culpa	my fault
memento mori	remember you have to die; a reminder of death, such as a skull
mirabile dictum	literally, wonderful to relate
mutatis mutandis	after making the necessary changes
nem. con., nemine contradicente	no one against; unanimously
non sequitur	it does not follow; an inference or conclusion that does not follow from its premises
op. cit., opere citato	in the work quoted; similar to loc. cit. (see above)
pace	despite
pari passu	on the same terms, at an equal pace or rate of progress
passim	adverb, here and there or scattered. Used in indexes to indicate that the item is scattered throughout the work and there are too many instances to enumerate them all
per se	by itself, for its own sake
persona non grata	person not in favour
per stirpes	among families; a lawyer's term used when distributing an inheritance
petitio elenchis	the sin of assuming a conclusion
post eventum	after the event
post hoc, ergo propter hoc	after this, therefore because of this. Used fallaciously in argument to show that because something comes after something it can be inferred that the first thing caused the second thing

post mortem	after death, used as an adjective and also as a noun, a clinical examination of a dead body
prima facie	from a first impression, apparently at first sight – no connection with love
primus inter pares	first among equals
pro tem., pro tempore	for the moment
PS, *post scriptum*	written afterwards
quid pro quo	something for something (or one thing for another), something in return, an equivalent
q.v., *quod vide*	which see; means that the reader should look for the word just mentioned (eg in glossary)
re	with regard to, in the matter of
sic	thus; used in brackets in quotes to show writer has made a mistake. "Mrs Thacher (sic) resigned today."
sine die	without (setting) a date
sine qua non	without which, not. Anything indispensable, and without which another cannot exist
status quo ante	the same state as before; usually shortened to status quo. A common usage is "maintaining the status quo"
stet	let it stand or do not delete; cancels an alteration in proofreading; dots are placed under what is to remain
sub judice	under judgment or consideration; not yet decided
sub rosa	under the rose, privately or furtively; not the same as under the gooseberry bush
ultra vires	beyond (one's) legal power
vade mecum	a little book or something carried about on the person; literally "Go with me"
vae victis	Woe to the conquered! A Roman phrase
versus, v or v.	against; used in legal cases and games
viz, videlicet	that is to say; to wit; namely

Laws

Scientific, economic, facetious and fatalistic laws in common use are listed here.

Boyle's law The pressure of a gas varies inversely with its volume at constant temperature.

Gresham's law When money of a high intrinsic value is in circulation with money of lesser value, it is the inferior currency which tends to remain in circulation, while the other is either hoarded or exported. In other words: "Bad money drives out good".

Grimm's law Concerns mutations of the consonants in the various Germanic languages. Proto-Indo-European voiced aspirated stops, voiced unaspirated stops and voiceless stops become respectively voiced unaspirated stops, voiceless stops and voiceless fricatives.

Heisenberg's uncertainty principle Energy and time or position and momentum cannot both be accurately measured simultaneously. The product of their uncertainties is h (Planck's constant).

Hooke's law The stress imposed on a solid is directly proportional to the strain produced within the elastic limit.

Laws of thermodynamics
1   The change in the internal energy of a system equals the sum of the heat added to the system and the work done on it.
2   Heat cannot be transferred from a colder to a hotter body within a system without net changes occurring in other bodies in the system.
3   It is impossible to reduce the temperature of a system to absolute zero in a finite number of steps.

Mendel's Principles The Law of Segregation is that every somatic cell of an individual carries a pair of hereditary units for each character: the pairs separate during meiosis so that each gamete carries one unit only of each pair.

The Law of Independent Assortment is that the separation of units of each pair is not influenced by that of any other pair.

Murphy's law Anything that can go wrong will go wrong. Also known as sod's law.

Ohm's law Electric current is directly proportional to electromotive force and inversely proportional to resistance.

Parkinson's law First published in *The Economist*, November 19th 1955. The author, C. Northcote Parkinson, sought to expand on the "commonplace observation that work expands so as to fill the time available for its completion". After studying Admiralty staffing levels, he concluded that in any public administrative department not actually at war the staff increase may be expected to follow this formula:

$$x = \frac{2k^m + p}{n}$$

Where k is the number of staff seeking promotion through the appointment of subordinates; p represents the difference between the ages of appointment and retirement; m is the number of hours devoted to answering minutes within the department; and n is the number of effective units being administered. Then x will be the number of new staff required each year.

Mathematicians will, of course, realise that to find the percentage increase they must multiply x by 100 and divide by the total of the previous year, thus:

$$\frac{100\,(2k^m + p)}{yn} \%$$

where y represents the total original staff. And this figure will invariably prove to be between 5.17% and 6.56%, irrespective of any variation in the amount of work (if any) to be done.

The Peter principle All members of a hierarchy rise to their own level of incompetence.

Say's law of markets A supply of goods generates a demand for the goods.

sod's law See **Murphy's law** on previous page.

Utz's laws of computer programming Any given program, when running, is obsolete. If a program is useful, it will have to be changed. Any given program will expand to fill all available memory.

Wolfe's law of journalism You cannot hope/to bribe or twist,/thank God! the/British journalist./But seeing what/the man will do/unbribed, there's/no occasion to.

Measures

UK imperial units

A change to the metric system has taken place in the UK, but dual labelling in imperial and metric is permitted by EU rules until end-2009.

The following imperial units may still be used in the UK after general conversion to the metric system: mile, yard, foot, inch for road traffic signs, distance and speed measurement; pint for draught beer and cider and for milk in returnable containers; acre for land registration; troy ounce for transactions in precious metals.

Conversions

Acceleration

Standard gravity	=	10 metres (m) per second squared
	=	32 feet (ft) per second squared

Volume and capacity

5 millilitres	=	1 teaspoonful
26 UK fluid oz	=	25 US liquid oz
$1^3/_4$ UK pints	=	1 litre (l)
5 UK pints	=	6 US liquid pints
9 US liquid pints	=	9l
5 UK gallons	=	6 US gallons
1 US gallon	=	$3^3/_4$l
3 cubic (cu.) ft	=	85 cu. decimetres
	=	85l
$27^1/_2$ UK bushels	=	1 cu. m
$28^1/_3$ US bushels	=	1 cu. m
11 UK bushels	=	4 hectolitres
14 US bushels	=	5 hectolitres
1 US bushel (heaped)	=	$1^1/_4$ US bushels (struck)
1 US dry barrel	=	$3^1/_4$ US bushels
1 US cranberry barrel	=	$2^3/_4$ bushels

1 barrel (petroleum)	=	42 US gallons
	=	35 UK gallons
1 barrel per day	=	50 tonnes per year

Weight

1 grain	=	65 milligrams
15 grains	=	1 gram (g)
11 ounces (oz)	=	10 oz troy
1 ounce	=	28g
1 oz troy	=	31g
1 pound (lb)	=	454g
35 oz	=	1 kilogram (kg)
2¼lb	=	1kg
11 US tons	=	10 tonnes
62 UK tons	=	63 tonnes
100 UK (long) tons	=	112 US (short) tons

Gold

The purity of gold is expressed as parts of 1,000, so that a fineness of 800 is 80% gold. Pure gold is defined as 24 carats (1,000 fine). Dental gold is usually 16 or 20 carat; gold in jewellery 9–22 carat. A golden sovereign is 22 carat.

1 metric carat = 200 milligrams.

Gold and silver are usually measured in troy weights: 1 troy ounce = 155.52 metric carats.

A standard international bar of gold is 400 troy ounces; bars of 250 troy ounces are also used.

Metric units

Metric units not generally recommended as SI units or for use with SI are marked with an asterisk (eg Calorie*).

Length

10 angstrom	=	1 nanometre
1,000 nanometres	=	1 micrometre
1,000 micrometres	=	1 millimetre (mm)
10mm	=	1 centimetre (cm)
10cm	=	1 decimetre
1,000mm	=	1 metre (m)
100cm	=	1m
10 decimetres	=	1m
100m	=	1 hectometre
10 hectometres	=	1 kilometre (km)

$$1{,}000\text{km} = 1 \text{ megametre}$$
$$\text{nautical: } 1{,}852\text{m} = 1 \text{ int. nautical mile}$$

Area

100 sq. mm	=	1 sq. cm
100 sq. cm	=	1 sq. decimetre
100 sq. decimetres	=	1 sq. m
100 sq. m	=	1 are
10,000 sq. m	=	1 hectare (ha)
100 ares	=	1 ha
100 ha	=	1 sq. kilometre

Weight (mass)

1,000 milligrams (mg)	=	1 gram (g)
1,000g	=	1 kilogram (kg)
100kg	=	1 quintal
1,000kg	=	1 tonne

Volume

1,000 cu. mm	=	1 cu. cm
1,000 cu. cm	=	1 cu. decimetre
1,000 cu. decimetres	=	1 cu. m

Capacity

10 millilitres (ml)	=	1 centilitre (cl)
10cl	=	1 decilitre (dl)
10dl	=	1 litre (l)
1l	=	1 cu. decimetre
100 litres	=	1hl
1,000l	=	1 kilolitre
10 hectolitres	=	1 kilolitre
1 kilolitre	=	1 cu. metre

Metric system prefixes

Prefix name	Symbol	Factor by which unit is multiplied		Description
atto	a	10^{-18} =	0.000 000 000 000 000 001	
femto	f	10^{-15} =	0.000 000 000 000 001	
pico	p	10^{-12} =	0.000 000 000 001	million millionth; trillionth
nano	n	10^{-9} =	0.000 000 001	thousand millionth; billionth
micro	μ	10^{-6} =	0.000 001	millionth
milli	m	10^{-3} =	0.001	thousandth

centi	c	10^{-2}	=	0.01	hundredth
deci	d	10^{-1}	=	0.1	tenth
deca (or deka)	da[a]	10^{1}	=	10	ten
hecto	h	10^{2}	=	100	hundred
kilo	k	10^{3}	=	1,000	thousand
myria	my	10^{4}	=	10,000	ten thousand
mega	M	10^{6}	=	1,000,000	million
giga	G	10^{9}	=	1,000,000,000	thousand million; billion
tera	T	10^{12}	=	1,000,000,000,000	million million; trillion
peta	P	10^{15}	=	1,000,000,000,000,000	
exa	E	10^{18}	=	1,000,000,000,000,000,000	

a Sometimes dk is used (eg, in Germany).

Units with different equivalents

Pound

UK, US avoirdupois pound (lb)	=	0.454kg
US: troy lb	=	0.373kg
	=	0.823lb (avoirdupois)
Spanish (libra)	=	0.460kg
	=	1.014lb (avoirdupois)
"Amsterdam"	=	0.494kg
	=	1.089lb (avoirdupois)
Danish (pund)	=	0.5kg
	=	1.102lb (avoirdupois)
Française (livre)	=	0.490kg
	=	1.079lb (avoirdupois)

Ton

UK: weight (mass)	=	2,240lb
	=	1.016 tonnes
shipping: register	=	100 cu. ft
	=	2.832 cu. m
US: short	=	2,000lb
	=	0.907 tonne
US: long	=	2,240lb
	=	1.016 tonnes
metric ton (tonne)	=	1,000kg
	=	2,204.62lb

Spanish: short (corta)	=	2,000 libras
	=	0.9202 tonne
	=	2,028.7lb
long (larga)	=	2,240 libras
	=	1.0306 tonnes
	=	2,272.1lb

Miscellaneous units and ratios

Beer, wines and spirits

	Proof (Sikes) (°)	Volume of alcohol (%)
Table wines	14-26	8-15
Port, sherry	26-38.5	15-22
Whisky, gin	65.5-70	37.5-40

Beer

small	=	half pint
large	=	1 pint
flagon	=	1 quart
anker	=	10 gallons

Wines and spirits

tot (whisky, gin, rum or vodka)	=	25ml or 35ml (before end-1994, one-sixth to one-quarter gill; the larger size is mainly used in Scotland)
wine glass	=	125ml or 175ml
wine bottle or carafe (metric sizes)	=	25cl, 50cl, 75cl or 1l

Champagne

2 bottles	=	1 magnum
4 bottles	=	1 jeroboam
20 bottles	=	1 nebuchadnezzar

Precious metals

1 metric carat	=	200mg
1 troy oz	=	155.52 metric carats

Crops

UK (imperial) bushel of

barley	=	50lb
maize	=	56lb
oats	=	39lb
potatoes	=	60lb
wheat	=	60lb
rye	=	56lb

US bushel as above except

barley	=	48lb
oats	=	32lb

Bale (cotton)

US (net)	=	480lb
Brazil	=	397lb (metric bale=180kg)
India	=	375lb (metric bale=170kg)

Extraction rates
Approximate weight ratios

100 grain	=	72 bread flour
100 paddy rice	=	67 milled rice
100 milk 4 butter		
1 ton barley	=	105 proof gal. whisky
Yield: 1 kg/ha	=	08922 lb/acre

Water
1l weighs 1 kg.
1 cubic m weighs 1 tonne.
1 UK gallon weighs 10.022lb.
1 US gallon weighs 8.345lb.

Energy

1 therm	=	29.3071 kilowatt hours (kW h)
1 terawatt hour (TW h)	=	1 thousand million kilowatt hours
1 watt second	=	1 joule
1 kilowatt hour	=	36 megajoules (MJ)
1 calorie (dieticians')	=	4.1855 kilojoules

Radioactivity

1 becquerel (Bq)	=	1 disintegration per sec.
1 rutherford	=	1m Bq

Dose of radiation

1 rad	=	10 millijoules per kg
1 gray	=	100 rad = 1 joule per kg
1 rem	=	1 rad, weighted by radiation effect
1 sievert (Sv)	=	100 rems
Background dose (UK)	=	25 millisievert (mSv) per year

Crude oil

1 barrel	=	42 US gallons
	=	34.97 UK (imperial) gallons
	=	0.159 cubic m (159l)
	=	0.136 tonne (approx.)
1 barrel per day (b/d)	=	50 tonnes per year (approx.)

Clothing sizes (rough equivalents)
Men's suits
UK/US	32	34	36	38	40	42	44
Europe	42	44	46	48	50	52	54
Metric	81	86	91	97	102	107	112

Women's suits, dresses, skirts
UK	10	12	14	16	18	20	22
US	8	10	12	14	16	18	20
Europe	38	40	42	44	47	50	52

Men's shirts (collar sizes)
UK/US (in)	15	15.5	16	16.5	17	17.5
Europe (cm)	38	39.5	41	42	43	44

Shoes
UK	5	6	7	8	9	10
US men's	6	7	8	9	10	11
US women's	6.5	7.5	8.5	9.5	10.5	11.5
Europe	38	39	40.5	42	43	44.5

Paper sizes
'A' Series (metric sizes)
A0 = 841mm × 1,189mm (33.11 in × 46.81 in)
A3 = 297mm × 420mm (11.69 in × 16.54 in)
A4 = 210mm × 297mm (8.27 in × 11.69 in)

'B' Series (metric sizes)
B0 = 1,000mm × 1,414mm (39.37 in × 55.67 in)
B4 = 250mm × 353mm (9.84 in × 13.90 in)

Conversion factors[a]

Multiply number of	by	to obtain equivalent number of
Length		
inches (in)	25.4	millimetres (mm)
inches	2.54	centimetres (cm)
feet (ft)	30.48	centimetres
feet	0.3048	metres (m)
yards (yd)	0.9144	metres
miles (land 5,280 ft)	1.609344	kilometres (km)
miles (UK sea)	1.853184	kilometres
miles, international nautical	1.852	kilometres
Area		
sq. inches (in²)	645.16	sq. millimetres (mm²)
sq. inches	6.4516	sq. centimetres (cm²)
sq. ft (ft²)	929.0304	sq. centimetres
sq. ft	0.092903	sq. metres (m²)
sq. yards (yd²)	0.836127	sq. metres
acres	4046.86	sq. metres
acres	0.404686	hectares (ha)
acres	0.004047	sq. kilometres (km²)
sq. miles	2.58999	sq. kilometres
Volume and capacity		
cu. inches (in³)	16.387064	cu. centimetres (cm3)
UK pints	34.6774	cu. inches
UK pints	0.5683	litres (l)
UK gallons	4.54609	litres
US gallons	3.785	litres
cu. feet (ft³)	28.317	litres
cu. feet	0.028317	cu. metres (cm³)
UK gallons	1.20095	US gallons
US gallons	0.832674	UK gallons

Multiply number of	by	to obtain equivalent number of
Length		
millimetres	0.03937	inches
centimetres	0.3937	inches
centimetres	0.03281	feet
metres	39.3701	inches
metres	3.2808	feet
metres	1.0936	yards
metres	0.54681	fathoms
kilometres	0.62137	miles (land)
kilometres	0.53961	miles (UK sea)
kilometres	0.53996	miles, international nautical
Area		
sq. millimetres	0.00155	sq. inches
sq. centimetres	0.1550	sq. inches
sq. metres	10.7639	sq. feet
sq. metres	1.19599	sq. yards
hectares	2.47105	acres
sq. kilometres	247.105	acres
sq. kilometres	0.3861	sq. miles
Volume and capacity		
cu. centimetres	0.06102	cu. inches
litres	61.024	cu. inches
litres	2.1134	US pints
litres	1.7598	UK pints
litres	0.2642	US gallons
litres	0.21997	UK gallons
hectolitres	26.417	US gallons
hectolitres	21.997	UK gallons
hectolitres	2.838	US bushels
hectolitres	2.750	UK bushels
cu. metres	35.3147	cu. feet
cu. metres	1.30795	cu. yards
cu. metres	264.172	US gallons

Multiply number of	by	to obtain equivalent number of
Weight (mass)		
ounces, avoirdupois (oz)	28.3495	grams (g)
ounces, troy (oz tr)	31.1035	grams
ounces, avoirdupois	0.9115	ounces, troy
pounds, avoirdupois (lb)	453.59237	grams
pounds, avoirdupois (lb)	0.45359	kilograms (kg)
short tons (2,000 lb)	0.892857	long tons
short tons (2,000 lb)	0.907185	tonnes (t)
long tons (2,240 lb)	1.12	short tons
long tons (2,240 lb)	1.01605	tonnes
Velocity and fuel consumption		
miles/hour	1.609344	kilometres/hour
miles/hour	0.868976	international knots
miles/UK gallon	0.35401	kilometres/litre
miles/US gallon	0.42514	kilometres/litre
UK gallons/mile[b]	282.481	litres/100 kilometres
US gallons/mile[b]	235.215	litres/100 kilometres
Temperature		
degrees Fahrenheit	5/9 after subtracting 32	degrees Celsius (centigrade)
-40°F	equals	-40°C
32°F	equals	0°C
59°F	equals	15°C

Multiply number of	by	to obtain equivalent number of
Weight (mass)		
grams	0.03527	ounces, avoirdupois
grams	0.03215	ounces, troy
kilograms	2.20462	pounds, avoirdupois
metric quintals (q)	220.462	pounds, avoirdupois
tonnes	2,204.62	pounds, avoirdupois
tonnes	1.10231	short tons
tonnes	0.984207	long tons
Velocity and fuel consumption		
kilometres/hour	0.62137	miles/hour
kilometres/hour	0.53996	international knots
kilometres/litre	2.82481	miles/UK gallon
litres/100 kilometres[c]	0.00354	UK gallons/mile
litres/100 kilometres[c]	0.00425	US gallons/mile
Temperature		
degrees Celsius	9/5 and add 32	degrees Fahrenheit
37°C	equals	98.6°F
50°C	equals	122°F
100°C	equals	212°F

a Between the UK and US systems, and the International System of Units (SI). As an example of the use of the table, 10 long tons (of 2,240lb each), multiplied by 1.12, is equal to 11.2 short tons (of 2,000lb each).
b Miles per UK gallon, divided into 282.481, gives litres per 100 kilometres; miles per US gallon, divided into 235.215, gives litres per 100 kilometres.
c Litres per 100 kilometres, divided into 282.481 gives miles per UK gallon; litres per 100 kilometres, divided into 235.215 gives miles per US gallon.

National accounts

These are the definitions adopted by the United Nations in 1968, but note that national accounts now refer to gross national product as gross national income (GNI).

Final expenditure

= private final consumption expenditure ("consumers' expenditure")
+ government final consumption expenditure
+ increase in stocks
+ gross fixed capital formation
+ exports of goods and services

Gross domestic product (GDP) at market prices

= final expenditure
− imports of goods and services

Gross national income or product (GNI/GNP) at market prices

= gross domestic product at market prices
+ net property income from other countries

Gross domestic product at factor cost

= gross domestic product at market prices
− indirect taxes
+ subsidies

Nobel Prize

This is an international award given each year since 1901 for achievements in physics, chemistry, medicine, literature and for peace. The Prize in Economic Sciences was instituted in 1968 by the Bank of Sweden. The winners are announced in October and receive their awards (cash, a gold medal and a diploma) on December 10th, the anniversary of Nobel's death. Here is a list of winners since 1990.

1990
Chemistry   Elias James Corey
Economics   Harry M. Markowitz, Merton H. Miller, William F. Sharpe
Literature Octavio Paz
Medicine   Joseph E. Murray, E. Donnall Thomas
Peace   Mikhail Gorbachev
Physics   Jerome I. Friedman, Henry W. Kendall, Richard E. Taylor

1991
Chemistry   Richard R. Ernst
Economics   Ronald H. Coase
Literature Nadine Gordimer
Medicine   Erwin Neher, Bert Sakmann
Peace   Aung San Suu Kyi
Physics   Pierre-Gilles de Gennes

1992
Chemistry   Rudolph A. Marcus
Economics   Gary S. Becker
Literature Derek Walcott
Medicine   Edmond H. Fischer, Edwin G. Krebs
Peace   Rigoberta Menchú Tum
Physics   Georges Charpak

1993
Chemistry   Kary B. Mullis, Michael Smith
Economics   Robert W. Fogel, Douglass C. North
Literature Toni Morrison
Medicine   Richard J. Roberts, Phillip A. Sharp
Peace   F.W. de Klerk, Nelson Mandela
Physics   Russell A. Hulse, Joseph H. Taylor Jr

1994
Chemistry   George A. Olah
Economics   John C. Harsanyi, John F. Nash Jr., Reinhard Selten
Literature Kenzaburo Oe
Medicine   Alfred G. Gilman, Martin Rodbell
Peace   Yasser Arafat, Shimon Peres, Yitzhak Rabin
Physics   Bertram N. Brockhouse, Clifford G. Shull

1995
Chemistry   Paul J. Crutzen, Mario J. Molina, F. Sherwood Rowland
Economics   Robert E. Lucas Jr
Literature Seamus Heaney

Medicine	Edward B. Lewis, Christiane Nüsslein-Volhard, Eric F. Wieschaus
Peace	Pugwash Conferences on Science and World Affairs, Joseph Rotblat
Physics	Martin L. Perl, Frederick Reines

1996

Chemistry	Robert F. Curl Jr., Sir Harold Kroto, Richard E. Smalley
Economics	James A. Mirrlees, William Vickrey
Literature	Wislawa Szymborska
Medicine	Peter C. Doherty, Rolf M. Zinkernagel
Peace	Carlos Filipe Ximenes Belo, José Ramos-Horta
Physics	David M. Lee, Douglas D. Osheroff, Robert C. Richardson

1997

Chemistry	Paul D. Boyer, Jens C. Skou, John E. Walker
Economics	Robert C. Merton, Myron S. Scholes
Literature	Dario Fo
Medicine	Stanley B. Prusiner
Peace	International Campaign to Ban Landmines, Jody Williams
Physics	Steven Chu, Claude Cohen-Tannoudji, William D. Phillips

1998

Chemistry	Walter Kohn, John Pople
Economics	Amartya Sen
Literature	José Saramago
Medicine	Robert F. Furchgott, Louis J. Ignarro, Ferid Murad
Peace	John Hume, David Trimble
Physics	Robert B. Laughlin, Horst L. Störmer, Daniel C. Tsui

1999

Chemistry	Ahmed Zewail
Economics	Robert A. Mundell
Literature	Günter Grass
Medicine	Günter Blobel
Peace	Médecins Sans Frontières
Physics	Gerardus 't Hooft, Martinus J.G. Veltman

2000

Chemistry	Alan Heeger, Alan G. MacDiarmid, Hideki Shirakawa
Economics	James J. Heckman, Daniel L. McFadden
Literature	Gao Xingjian
Medicine	Arvid Carlsson, Paul Greengard, Eric R. Kandel
Peace	Kim Dae-jung

Physics	Zhores I. Alferov, Jack S. Kilby, Herbert Kroemer

2001

Chemistry	William S. Knowles, Ryoji Noyori, K. Barry Sharpless
Economics	George A. Akerlof, A. Michael Spence, Joseph E. Stiglitz
Literature	V.S. Naipaul
Medicine	Leland H. Hartwell, Tim Hunt, Sir Paul Nurse
Peace	United Nations, Kofi Annan
Physics	Eric A. Cornell, Wolfgang Ketterle, Carl E. Wieman

2002

Chemistry	John B. Fenn, Kurt Wüthrich, Koichi Tanaka
Economics	Daniel Kahneman, Vernon L. Smith
Literature	Imre Kertész
Medicine	Sydney Brenner, Robert Horvitz, John E. Sulston
Peace	Jimmy Carter
Physics	Raymond Davis Jr., Riccardo Giacconi, Masatoshi Koshiba

2003

Chemistry	Peter Agre, Roderick MacKinnon
Economics	Robert F. Engle III, Clive W.J. Granger
Literature	J.M. Coetzee
Medicine	Paul C. Lauterbur, Sir Peter Mansfield
Peace	Shirin Ebadi
Physics	Alexei A. Abrikosov, Vitaly L. Ginzburg, Anthony J. Leggett

2004

Chemistry	Aaron Ciechanover, Avram Hershko, Irwin Rose
Economics	Finn E. Kydland, Edward C. Prescott
Literature	Elfriede Jelinek
Medicine	Richard Axel, Linda B. Buck
Peace	Wangari Maathai
Physics	David J. Gross, David Politzer, Frank Wilczek

Olympic games

I	Athens	1896	XVI	Melbourne	1956
II	Paris	1900	XVII	Rome	1960
III	St Louis	1904	XVIII	Tokyo	1964
IV	London	1908	XIX	Mexico City	1968
V	Stockholm	1912	XX	Munich	1972
VI	Berlin (cancelled)	1916	XXI	Montreal	1976
VII	Antwerp	1920	XXII	Moscow	1980
VIII	Paris	1924	XXIII	Los Angeles	1984
IX	Amsterdam	1928	XXIV	Seoul	1988
X	Los Angeles	1932	XXV	Barcelona	1992
XI	Berlin	1936	XXVI	Atlanta	1996
XII	Tokyo/Helsinki (cancelled)	1940	XXVII	Sydney	2000
			XXVIII	Athens	2004
XIII	London (cancelled)	1944	XXIX	Beijing	2008
XIV	London	1948	XXX	London	2012
XV	Helsinki	1952			

Organisations

These are the exact names and abbreviated titles of the main international organisations. Where membership is small or exclusive, members are listed too.

African Union formerly the Organization of African Unity (OAU), founded in 1962, headquarters in Addis Ababa, Ethiopia.

Members

Algeria	Cameroon	Congo (Brazzaville)
Angola	Cape Verde	Congo, Democratic
Benin	Central African	Republic of
Botswana	Republic	Côte d'Ivoire
Burkina Faso	Chad	Djibouti
Burundi	Comoros	Egypt

Equatorial Guinea	Mali	Seychelles
Eritrea	Mauritania	Sierra Leone
Ethiopia	Mauritius	Somalia
Gabon	Mozambique	South Africa
The Gambia	Namibia	Sudan
Ghana	Niger	Swaziland
Guinea Bissau	Nigeria	Tanzania
Guinea Conakry	Rwanda	Togo
Kenya	Saharawi Arab	Tunisia
Lesotho	Democratic	Uganda
Liberia	Republic	Zambia
Libya	São Tomé and	Zimbabwe
Madagascar	Principe	
Malawi	Senegal	

ALADI Asociación Latinoamericana de Integración (Latin American Integration Association), founded in 1980, based in Montevideo, Uruguay.

Members[a]

Argentina	Colombia	Paraguay
Bolivia	Cuba	Peru
Brazil	Ecuador	Uruguay
Chile	Mexico	Venezuela

a There are also 16 observer countries and nine observer organisations.

Andean Community of Nations founded in 1969, headquarters in Lima, Peru.

Members

Bolivia	Ecuador	Venezuela
Colombia	Peru	

APEC Asia-Pacific Economic Cooperation, founded in 1989, based in Singapore.

Members

Australia	Japan	Russia
Brunei	Malaysia	Singapore
Canada	Mexico	South Korea
Chile	New Zealand	Taiwan
China	Papua New Guinea	Thailand
Hong Kong SAR	Peru	US
Indonesia	Philippines	Vietnam

ASEAN Association of South-east Asian Nations, established in 1967, headquarters in Jakarta, Indonesia.

Members

Brunei	Malaysia	Singapore
Cambodia	Myanmar	Thailand
Indonesia	Philippines	Vietnam
Laos		

BIS Bank for International Settlements, the central bankers' central bank, founded 1930, based in Basel, Switzerland.

Members[a]

Algeria	Greece	Poland
Argentina	Hong Kong SAR	Portugal
Australia	Hungary	Romania
Austria	Iceland	Russia
Belgium	India	Saudi Arabia
Bosnia & Hercegovina	Indonesia	Singapore
Brazil	Ireland	Slovakia
Bulgaria	Israel	Slovenia
Canada	Italy	South Africa
Chile	Japan	South Korea
China	Latvia	Spain
Croatia	Lithuania	Sweden
Czech Republic	Macedonia	Switzerland
Denmark	Malaysia	Thailand
Estonia	Mexico	Turkey
Finland	Netherlands	UK
France	Norway	US
Germany	Philippines	

a   The European Central Bank is a shareholder.

CARICOM Caribbean Community and Common Market, formed in 1973, secretariat in Georgetown, Guyana.

Members

Anguilla[a]	Cayman Islands[a]	St Kitts-Nevis
Antigua and Barbuda	Dominica	St Lucia
Bahamas[b]	Grenada	St Vincent and the Grenadines
Barbados	Guyana	Suriname
Belize	Haiti	Trinidad and Tobago
Bermuda[a]	Jamaica	Turks and Caicos Islands[a]
British Virgin Islands[a]	Montserrat	

a   Associate member.
b   Member of the Community but not the Common Market.

Observer status

Aruba	Netherlands Antilles
Colombia	Puerto Rico
Dominican Republic	Venezuela
Mexico	

COMESA Common Market for Eastern and Southern Africa, founded in 1993, headquarters in Lusaka, Zambia.

Members

Angola	Eritrea	Rwanda
Burundi	Ethiopia	Seychelles
Comoros	Kenya	Sudan
Congo, Democratic	Madagascar	Swaziland
Republic of	Malawi	Uganda
Djibouti	Mauritius	Zambia
Egypt	Namibia	Zimbabwe

Commonwealth based in London, UK.

Members

Antigua	Kenya	Samoa
and Barbuda	Kiribati	Seychelles
Australia	Lesotho	Sierra Leone[c]
Bahamas	Malawi	Singapore
Bangladesh	Malaysia	Solomon Islands
Barbados	Maldives	South Africa[d]
Belize	Malta	Sri Lanka
Botswana	Mauritius	Swaziland
Brunei	Mozambique	Tanzania
Cameroon	Namibia	Tonga
Canada	Nauru	Trinidad and Tobago
Cyprus	New Zealand	Tuvalu
Dominica	Nigeria[a]	Uganda
Fiji	Pakistan[b]	UK
The Gambia	Papua New Guinea	Vanuatu
Ghana	St Kitts-Nevis	Zambia
Grenada	St Lucia	
Guyana	St Vincent and	
India	the Grenadines	
Jamaica		

a Suspended in November 1995, but reinstated in May 1999.
b Suspended in late 1999, but reinstated in 2004.
c Suspended in 1997, but subsequently reinstated.
d Withdrew in 1961, but rejoined in 1994.

Dependencies and associated states

Australia

Ashmore and Cartier Islands	Coral Sea Islands Territory
Australian Antarctic Territory	Heard and McDonald Islands
Christmas Island	Norfolk Island
Cocos (Keeling) Islands	

New Zealand

Cook Islands	Ross Dependency
Niue	Tokelau

UK

Anguilla	Channel Islands	South Georgia and
Bermuda	Falkland Islands	South Sandwich Islands
British Antarctic	Gibraltar	Tristan da Cunha
Territory	Isle of Man	Turks and
British Indian	Montserrat	Caicos Islands
Ocean Territory	Pitcairn Islands –	
British Virgin Islands	St Helena, Ascension	
Cayman Islands		

Commonwealth of Independent States (CIS) founded by the former Soviet Socialist Republics in December 1991, based in Moscow, Russia.

Members

Armenia	Kazakhstan	Tajikistan
Azerbaijan	Kirgizstan	Turkmenistan
Belarus	Moldova	Ukraine
Georgia	Russia	Uzbekistan

ECOWAS Economic Community of West African States, founded 1975, secretariat in Abuja, Nigeria.

Members

Benin	Ghana	Niger
Burkina Faso	Guinea	Nigeria
Cape Verde	Guinea-Bissau	Senegal
Côte d'Ivoire	Liberia	Sierra Leone
The Gambia	Mali	Togo

EEA European Economic Area, negotiated in 1992 between the European Community and members of EFTA, came into force in 1994 and has been maintained because the three signatories – Iceland, Norway and Liechtenstein – wanted to participate in the Single Market without being full members of the EU.

EFTA European Free Trade Association, established 1960.

Members

Iceland	Norway
Liechtenstein	Switzerland

EU European Union, the collective designation of three organisations with common membership: the European Coal and Steel Community (ECSC, treaty expired in 2002), European Economic Community (EEC) and European Atomic Energy Community (EURATOM). They merged to become the European Community (EC) in 1967. In November 1993 when the Maastricht treaty came into force the EC was incorporated into the EU. Economic and Monetary Union (EMU) formed one of the articles of the Maastricht treaty, in which were set out the stages by which the EU would progress to full convergence, with a single currency, the euro. Headquarters in Brussels, with some activities in Luxembourg and Strasbourg.

Main institutions

European Commission	Committee of the Regions
Council of Ministers	Court of Justice
European Council	Court of Auditors
European Parliament	European Investment Bank (EIB)
Economic and Social Committee (ESC)	

Other bodies

European Agency for the Evaluation of Medicinal Products (EMEA)	European Foundation for the Improvement of Living and Working Conditions
European Environment Agency (EEA)	Office for Harmonisation in the Internal Market (OHIM)
European Training Foundation	Community Plant Variety Rights Office
European Centre for the Development of Vocational Training (CEDEFOP)	European Agency for Safety and Health at Work
European Centre for Drugs and Drug Addiction (EMCDDA)	Translation Centre for Bodies in the European Union

Members

Austria (1994)	Denmark (1973)	Germany[a]
Belgium[a]	Estonia (2004)	Greece (1981)
Cyprus (2004)	Finland (1994)	Hungary (2004)
Czech Republic (2004)	France[a]	Ireland (1973)

Italy[a]	Netherlands[a]	Spain (1986)
Latvia (2004)	Poland (2004)	Sweden (1994)
Lithuania (2004)	Portugal (1986)	UK (1973)
Luxembourg[a]	Slovakia (2004)	
Malta (2004)	Slovenia (2004)	

a Founding member.
Note: Year of joining in brackets.

Franc Zone Comité Monétaire de la Zone Franc.

Members

Benin[a]	Congo, Democratic	Mali[a]
Burkina Faso[a]	Côte d'Ivoire[a]	Niger[a]
Cameroon[b]	Equatorial Guinea[b]	Senegal[a]
Central African Republic[b]	French Overseas Territories[c]	Togo[a]
Chad[b]	Gabon[b]	
Comoros[b]	Guinea-Bissau[a]	

a Member of Banque Centrale des Etats de l'Afrique de l'Ouest.
b Member of Banque des Etats de l'Afrique Centrale.
c New Caledonia, French Polynesia and the Wallis and Futuna Islands.

FTAA Free Trade Area of the Americas, set up in November 2002 to integrate the economies of the western hemisphere into a single free trade agreement.

Members

Antigua & Barbuda	Dominican Republic	Paraguay
Argentina	Ecuador	Peru
Bahamas	El Salvador	St Kitts & Nevis
Barbados	Grenada	St Lucia
Belize	Guatemala	St Vincent &
Bolivia	Guyana	the Grenadines
Brazil	Haiti	Suriname
Canada	Honduras	Trinidad & Tobago
Chile	Jamaica	US
Colombia	Mexico	Uruguay
Costa Rica	Nicaragua	Venezuela
Dominica	Panama	

GCC Co-operation Council for the Arab States of the Gulf or Gulf Co-operation Council, established in 1981, headquarters in Riyadh, Saudi Arabia.

Members

Bahrain	Oman	Saudi Arabia
Kuwait	Qatar	United Arab Emirates

G7, G8, G10, G22, G26 In 1975, six countries, the world's leading capitalist countries, ranked by GDP, were represented in France at the first annual summit meeting: the US, the UK, Germany, Japan and Italy, as well as the host country. The following year they were joined by Canada and, in 1977, by representatives of the European Union, although the group continued to be known as the G7. At the 1989 summit, 15 developing countries were also represented, although this did not give birth to the G22, which was not set up until 1998 and swiftly grew into G26. At the 1991 G7 summit, a meeting was held with the Soviet Union, a practice that continued (with Russia) in later years. In 1998, although it was not one of the world's eight richest countries, Russia became a full member of the G8. Meetings of the IMF are attended by the G10, which includes 11 countries.

G10 members

Belgium	Italy	Switzerland
Canada	Japan	UK
France	Netherlands	US
Germany	Sweden	

IATA International Air Transport Association, head offices in Montreal and Geneva; regional offices in Miami and Singapore.

Members: most international airlines

International Seabed Authority an autonomous organisation in relationship with the UN, established 1996, based in Kingston, Jamaica
Members: 148 signatories to the Convention on the Law of the Sea.

Mercosur Mercado Común del Sur (Southern Common Market), founded in 1991, based in Montevideo, Uruguay.

Members	*Associate members*
Argentina	Bolivia
Brazil	Chile
Paraguay	
Uruguay	

NATO North Atlantic Treaty Organisation, an alliance of 26 countries from Europe and North America committed to fulfilling goals of North Atlantic Treaty signed on April 4th 1949; headquarters in Brussels, Belgium.

Members

Belgium	Czech Republic	France
Bulgaria	Denmark	Germany
Canada	Estonia	Greece

Hungary	Netherlands	Slovenia
Iceland	Norway	Spain
Italy	Poland	Turkey
Latvia	Portugal	UK
Lithuania	Romania	US
Luxembourg	Slovakia	

OAS Organization of American States, formed in 1948, headquarters in Washington, DC.

Members[a][b]

Antigua and Barbuda	Dominica	Panama
	Dominican Republic	Paraguay
Argentina	Ecuador	Peru
Bahamas	El Salvador	St Kitts-Nevis
Barbados	Grenada	St Lucia
Belize	Guatemala	St Vincent and the Grenadines
Bolivia	Guyana	Suriname
Brazil	Haiti	Trinidad and Tobago
Canada	Honduras	US
Chile	Jamaica	Uruguay
Colombia	Mexico	Venezuela
Costa Rica	Nicaragua	

a Has many permanent non-member observers.
b Cuba has been excluded from participation in the OAS since 1962.

OECD Organisation for Economic Co-operation and Development, capitalism's club, founded in 1961, based in Paris, France. The European Commission also takes part in the OECD's work.

Members

Australia	Hungary	Poland
Austria	Iceland	Portugal
Belgium	Ireland	Slovakia
Canada	Italy	South Korea
Czech Republic	Japan	Spain
Denmark	Luxembourg	Sweden
Finland	Mexico	Switzerland
France	Netherlands	Turkey
Germany	New Zealand	UK
Greece	Norway	US

OPEC Organization of the Petroleum Exporting Countries, established 1960, based in Vienna, Austria.

Members

Algeria	Kuwait	Saudi Arabia
Indonesia	Libya	United Arab Emirates
Iran	Nigeria	Venezuela
Iraq	Qatar	

OSCE Organization for Security and Co-operation in Europe, originally founded in 1972 as the Conference on Security and Co-operation in Europe (CSCE).

Members: 55, including European countries, Canada, the US and former republics of the Soviet Union

SADC Southern African Development Community, replaced the Southern African Co-ordination Conference in 1992, based in Gaborone, Botswana. Its aim is to work for development and economic growth in the region with common systems and institutions, promoting peace and security, and achieving complementary national and regional strategies.

Members

Angola	Malawi	South Africa
Botswana	Mauritius	Swaziland
Congo, Democratic	Mozambique	Tanzania
Republic of	Namibia	Zambia
Lesotho	Seychelles	Zimbabwe

The United Nations (UN) officially came into existence on October 24th 1945, based in New York, US.

General Assembly	Trusteeship Council
Security Council	International Court of Justice
Economic and Social Council (ECOSOC)	

Secretaries-general

Sir Gladwyn Jebb (UK), acting, 1945-46

Trygve Lie (Norway), February 1946 to his resignation in November 1952

Dag Hammarskjöld (Sweden), April 1953 until his death in a plane crash in Northern Rhodesia (now Zambia), September 1961

U Thant (Burma, now Myanmar), November 1961-December 1971

Kurt Waldheim (Austria) 1972-81

Javier Pérez de Cuéllar (Peru) 1982-91

Boutros Boutros-Ghali (Egypt), January 1992 to the American veto of his second term in December 1996

Kofi Annan (Ghana), January 1997 to present

Regional commissions		*Head office*
Economic Commission for Africa	ECA	Addis Ababa
Economic Commission for Europe	ECE	Geneva
Economic Commission for Latin America and the Caribbean	ECLAC	Santiago, Chile
Economic and Social Commission for Asia and the Pacific	ESCAP	Bangkok
Economic and Social Commission for Western Asia	ESCWA	Beirut

Other UN bodies		
Department of Peace-keeping Operations	DPKO	New York
Office for the Co-ordination of Humanitarian Affairs	OCHA	New York
Office of United Nations High Commissioner for Human Rights	OHCHR	Geneva
United Nations Human Settlements Programme	UNHSP (UN-Habitat)	Nairobi
United Nations Children's Fund	UNICEF	New York
United Nations Conference on Trade and Development	UNCTAD	Geneva
United Nations Development Programme	UNDP	New York
United Nations Environment Programme	UNEP	Nairobi
United Nations High Commissioner for Refugees	UNHCR	Geneva
United Nations Office on Drugs and Crime	UNODC	Vienna
United Nations Population Fund	UNFPA	New York
United Nations Relief and Works Agency for Palestine Refugees in the Near East	UNRWA	Gaza City, Amman
United Nations Institute for Research and Training	UNITAR	Geneva
World Food Programme	WFP	Rome

Specialised agencies within the UN system

Food and Agriculture Organization	FAO	Rome
International Atomic Energy Agency	IAEA	Vienna
International Civil Aviation Organization	ICAO	Montreal
International Fund for Agricultural Development	IFAD	Rome
International Labour Organization	ILO	Geneva
International Maritime Organization	IMO	London
International Monetary Fund	IMF	Washington, DC
International Telecommunications Union	ITU	Geneva
Multilateral Investment Guarantee Agency	MIGA	Washington, DC
United Nations Educational, Scientific and Cultural Organization	UNESCO	Paris
United Nations Industrial Development Organization	UNIDO	Vienna
Universal Postal Union	UPU	Bern
World Bank[a]		Washington, DC
World Health Organization	WHO	Geneva
World Intellectual Property Organization	WIPO	Geneva
World Meteorological Organization	WMO	Geneva

a Comprising the International Bank for Reconstruction and Development (IBRD), the International Finance Corporation (IFC), the International Development Association (IDA) and the Multilateral Investment Guarantee Agency (MIGA).

WTO World Trade Organisation, the international organisation of the world trading system with co-operative links to the UN, established in 1995 as successor to the General Agreement on Tariffs and Trade (GATT), based in Geneva.

Members: 148 countries

Populations of the world

Here are the countries of the world with populations of at least 1m, showing their areas, capitals and GDP.

Country	Population (m)	Area (000 sq km)	Capital	GDP ($bn)
China	1,304.2	9,561	Beijing	1,417.0
India	1,065.5	3,287	New Delhi	600.6
US	294.0	9,373	Washington, DC	10,949.0
Indonesia	219.9	1,904	Jakarta	208.3
Brazil	178.5	8,512	Brasilia	412.0
Pakistan	153.6	804	Islamabad	82.3
Bangladesh	146.7	144	Dhaka	51.9
Russia	143.2	17,075	Moscow	432.9
Japan	127.7	378	Tokyo	4,301.0
Nigeria	124.0	924	Abuja	58.4
Mexico	103.5	1,973	Mexico City	626.1
Germany	82.5	358	Berlin	2,403.0
Vietnam	81.4	331	Hanoi	39.2
Philippines	80.0	300	Manila	80.6
Egypt	71.9	1,000	Cairo	82.4
Iran	68.9	1,648	Tehran	137.1
Turkey	71.3	779	Ankara	240.4
Thailand	62.8	513	Bangkok	143.0
France	60.1	544	Paris	1,758.0
UK	59.3	243	London	1,795.0
Italy	57.4	301	Rome	1,468.0
Ukraine	48.5	604	Kiev	49.5
South Korea	47.7	99	Seoul	605.3
South Africa	45.0	1,226	Pretoria	159.9
Colombia	44.2	1,142	Bogotá	78.7
Spain	41.1	505	Madrid	838.7
Poland	38.6	313	Warsaw	209.6
Argentina	38.4	2,767	Buenos Aires	130.0
Kenya	32.0	583	Nairobi	14.4

Country	Population (m)	Area (000 sq km)	Capital	GDP ($bn)
Algeria	31.8	2,382	Algiers	66.5
Canada	31.5	9,971	Ottawa	857.0
Morocco	30.6	447	Rabat	43.7
Peru	27.2	1,285	Lima	60.6
Venezuela	25.7	912	Caracas	85.4
Malaysia	24.4	333	Kuala Lumpur	103.7
Saudia Arabia	24.2	2,200	Riyadh	214.7
Taiwan	22.6	36	Taipei	286.2
Romania	22.3	238	Bucharest	57.0
Australia	19.7	7,682	Canberra	522.0
Côte D'Ivoire	16.6	322	Abidjan/ Yamoussoukro	13.7
Netherlands	16.1	42	Amsterdam	511.5
Cameroon	16.0	757	Santiago	72.4
Chile	15.8	475	Yaoundé	12.5
Zimbabwe	12.9	391	Harare	8.3
Greece	11.0	132	Athens	172.2
Belgium	10.3	31	Brussels	302.0
Czech Republic	10.2	79	Prague	89.7
Portugal	10.1	89	Lisbon	147.9
Hungary	9.9	93	Budapest	82.7
Sweden	8.9	450	Stockholm	301.6
Austria	8.1	84	Vienna	253.0
Bulgaria	7.9	111	Sofia	19.9
Switzerland	7.2	41	Berne	320.1
Israel	6.4	21	Jerusalem	110.2
Denmark	5.4	43	Copenhagen	211.9
Slovakia	5.4	49	Bratislava	32.5
Finland	5.2	338	Helsinki	161.9
Norway	4.5	324	Oslo	220.9
Singapore	4.3	>1	Singapore	91.3
Ireland	4.0	70	Dublin	153.7
New Zealand	3.9	271	Wellington	79.6
Lithuania	3.4	65	Vilnius	18.2
United Arab Emirates	3.0	84	Abu Dhabi	71.0
Latvia	2.3	64	Riga	11.1
Slovenia	2.0	20	Ljubljana	27.7
Estonia	1.3	45	Tallinn	9.1

Source: *The Economist Pocket World in Figures* 2006, Profile Books, London, 2005.

Presidents of the US and prime ministers of the UK

Here are lists of presidents of America and prime ministers of the UK.

Presidents of the United States

Date	President	Date	President
1789-97	George Washington	1889-93	Benjamin Harrison
1797-1801	John Adams	1893-97	Grover Cleveland
1801-09	Thomas Jefferson	1897-1901	William McKinley
1809-17	James Madison	1901-09	Theodore Roosevelt
1817-25	James Monroe	1909-13	William H. Taft
1825-29	John Adams	1913-21	Woodrow Wilson
1829-37	Andrew Jackson	1921-23	Warren Harding
1837-41	Martin Van Buren	1923-29	Calvin Coolidge
1841	William Henry Harrison	1929-33	Herbert Hoover
1841-45	John Tyler	1933-45	Franklin D. Roosevelt
1845-49	James Polk	1945-53	Harry Truman
1849-50	Zachary Taylor	1953-61	Dwight Eisenhower
1850-53	Millard Fillmore	1961-63	John F. Kennedy
1853-57	Franklin Pierce	1963-69	Lyndon Johnson
1857-61	James Buchanan	1969-74	Richard Nixon
1861-65	Abraham Lincoln	1974-77	Gerald Ford
1865-69	Andrew Johnson	1977-81	Jimmy Carter
1869-77	Ulysses S. Grant	1981-89	Ronald Reagan
1877-81	Rutherford B. Hayes	1989-93	George H.W. Bush
1881	James Garfield	1993-2001	William J. Clinton
1881-85	Chester Arthur	2001-	George W. Bush
1885-89	Grover Cleveland		

Prime ministers of the United Kingdom

Date	Prime minister
1721-42	Sir Robert Walpole
1742-43	Spencer Compton, Earl of Wilmington
1743-54	Henry Pelham
1754-56	Thomas Pelham-Holles, Duke of Newcastle
1756-57	William Cavendish, Duke of Devonshire
1757	James Waldegrave, 2nd Earl Waldegrave
1757-62	Thomas Pelham Holles, Duke of Newcastle
1762-63	John Stuart, Earl of Bute
1763-65	George Grenville
1765-66	Charles Wentworth, Marquess of Rockingham

Date	Prime minister
1766-68	Earl of Chatham, William Pitt "The Elder"
1768-70	Augustus Henry Fitzroy, Duke of Grafton
1770-82	Lord North
1782	Charles Wentworth, Marquess of Rockingham
1782-83	William Petty, Earl of Shelburne
1783	William Henry Cavendish Bentinck, 3rd Duke of Portland
1783-1801	William Pitt "The Younger"
1801-04	Henry Addington
1804-06	William Pitt "The Younger"
1806-07	William Wyndam Grenville, Lord Grenville
1807-09	William Henry Cavendish Bentinck, 3rd Duke of Portland
1809-12	Spencer Perceval
1812-27	Robert Banks Jenkinson, Earl of Liverpool
1827	George Canning
1827-28	Frederick Robinson, Viscount Goderich
1828-30	Arthur Wellesley, Duke of Wellington
1830-34	Earl Grey
1834	William Lamb, Viscount Melbourne
1834-35	Sir Robert Peel
1835-41	William Lamb, Viscount Melbourne
1841-46	Sir Robert Peel
1846-52	Earl Russell
1852	Earl of Derby
1852-55	Earl of Aberdeen
1855-58	Viscount Palmerston
1858-59	Earl of Derby
1859-65	Viscount Palmerston
1865-66	Earl Russell
1866-68	Earl of Derby
1868	Benjamin Disraeli
1868-74	William Ewart Gladstone
1874-80	Benjamin Disraeli
1880-85	William Ewart Gladstone
1885-86	Robert Arthur Talbot Gascoyne-Cecil, Marquess of Salisbury
1886	William Ewart Gladstone
1886-92	Robert Arthur Talbot Gascoyne-Cecil, Marquess of Salisbury
1892-94	William Ewart Gladstone
1894-95	Earl of Rosebery
1895-1902	Robert Arthur Talbot Gascoyne-Cecil, Marquess of Salisbury
1902-05	Arthur James Balfour

Date	Prime minister
1905-08	Sir Henry Campbell-Bannerman
1908-16	Herbert Henry Asquith
1916-22	David Lloyd George
1922-23	Andrew Bonar Law
1923	Stanley Baldwin
1924	James Ramsay MacDonald
1924-29	Stanley Baldwin
1929-35	James Ramsay MacDonald
1935-37	Stanley Baldwin
1937-40	Neville Chamberlain
1940-45	Sir Winston Churchill
1945-51	Clement Richard Attlee
1951-55	Sir Winston Churchill
1955-57	Sir Anthony Eden
1957-63	Harold Macmillan
1963-64	Sir Alec Douglas-Home
1964-70	Harold Wilson
1970-74	Edward Heath
1974-76	Harold Wilson
1976-79	James Callaghan
1979-90	Margaret Thatcher
1990-97	John Major
1997-	Tony Blair

Proofreading

Look for errors in the following categories:

1 "Typos", which include misspelt words, punctuation mistakes, wrong numbers and transposed words or sentences.
2 Bad word breaks.
3 Layout mistakes: wrongly positioned text (including captions, headings, folios, running heads) or illustrations, incorrect line spacing, missing items, widows (pages that begin with the last word or line of a paragraph – they have a past but no future), orphans (paragraphs that begin on the last line of a page – they have no past but they do have a future).
4 Wrong fonts: errors in the use of italic, bold, typeface (eg, Arial not Times New Roman), etc.

If the text contains cross-references to numbered pages or

illustrations, the proofreader is often responsible for inserting the correct reference at page proof stage, and for checking cross-references.

The most effective way of proofreading is to read the text several times, each time with a different aim in mind, rather than attempting to carry out all checks in one go.

proofreading marks are illustrated on pages 233ff. (The full set of proofreading marks is defined by British Standard BS 5261 "Copy preparation and proof correction".) The intention of these marks is to identify, precisely and concisely, the nature of an error and the correction required. When corrections are extensive or complex, it is usually better to spell out in full the correct form of the text rather than leave the typesetter to puzzle over a string of hieroglyphs, however immaculately drawn and ordered. Mark all proof corrections clearly and write them in the margin.

word breaks It may be necessary to break words, using a hyphen, at the end of lines. Computer word-processing programs come with standard hyphenation rules but these can always be changed or overruled. Ideally, the aim should be to make these breaks as undisruptive as possible, so that the reader does not stumble or falter. Whenever possible, the word should be broken so that, helped by the context, the reader can anticipate the whole word from the part of it given before the break. Here are some useful principles for deciding how to break a word.

1. Words that are already hyphenated should be broken at the hyphen, not given a second hyphen.
2. Words can be broken according to either their derivation (the British convention) or their pronunciation (the US convention): thus, *aristo-cracy* (UK) or *aristoc-racy* (US), *melli-fluous* (UK) or *mellif-luous* (US). (*See* Part 2 for American usage.)
3. Words of one syllable should not be broken.
4. Words of five or fewer characters should not be broken.
5. At least three characters must be taken over to the next line.
6. Words should not be broken so that their identity is confused or their identifying sound is distorted: thus, avoid *wo-men*, *fo-ist*, *the-rapist*.
7. Personal names and acronyms (eg, NATO) should not be broken.
8. Figures should not be broken or separated from their unit of measurement.

9   A word formed with a prefix or suffix should be broken at that point: thus, *bi-furcated, ante-diluvian, convert-ible.*

10 If a breakable word contains a double consonant, split it at that point: thus, *as-sess, ship-ping, prob-lem.*

11 Do not hyphenate the last word on the right-hand page.

INSTRUCTION	TEXTUAL MARK	MARGINAL MARK AND NOTES
Correction is concluded	None	/ Make after each correction
Leave unchanged	••••• under characters to remain	✓ (circled)
Insert in text the matter indicated in the margin	⋏ (caret mark)	New matter followed by ⋏
Delete	/ through character(s) or ⊢——⊣ through words	∂|
Delete and close up	⌐/ through character(s) or ⊢====⊣ through characters, eg, o/r, charac⌐ter	∂| (with close-up curve)
Close up – delete space	⌒ (close up)	⌒ (close up)
Substitute character or substitute part of one or more words	through / character or ⊢——⫠ through words	new character or new word(s)
Wrong font. Replace with correct font	Encircle character(s) to be changed	⊗ or w.f.
Set in or change to roman type	Encircle character(s) to be changed	Rom.
Set in or change to italic	——— under character(s) to be set or changed	⊔⊔

INSTRUCTION	TEXTUAL MARK	MARGINAL MARK AND NOTES
Set in or change to capital letters	≡≡≡ under character(s) to be set or changed	≡
Set in or change to small capital letters	 ≡≡ under character(s) to be set or changed	=
Set in or change to bold type	∿∿∿ under character(s) to be set or changed	∿∿ or bold
Set in or change to bold italic type	 ∿∿∿ under character(s) to be set or changed	 ⨧
Change capital letters to lower case letters	Encircle character(s) to be changed	≢ or l.c.
Change italic to upright type	Encircle character(s) to be changed	 ⨧
Invert type	Encircle character to be changed	 ↻
Substitute or insert character in "superior" position	╱ through character or ∧ where required	� mark under character eg  ╱₂
Substitute or insert full stop or decimal point	╱ through character or ∧ where required	⊙
Substitute or insert comma	╱ through character or ∧ where required	،

234

INSTRUCTION	TEXTUAL MARK	MARGINAL MARK AND NOTES
Substitute or insert colon	/ through character or ⋏ where required	⊙
Insert hyphen	/ through character or ⋏ where required	⊢-⊣
Substitute or insert semi-colon	/ through character or ⋏ where required	;
Insert space	⋏ or /	⊺
Equal space	| between words or letters	⊼
Reduce space	⌒| between words or letters	⌒
Start new paragraph	⌐	⌐
Run on (no new paragraph)	⌒	⌒
Transpose characters or words	⌐⌐ between characters or words, numbered when necessary	⌐⌐
Transpose lines	⊐	⊐
Indent	⊏	⊏
Move to the left	|←[xxxx]	⊐
Insert single or double quotes	⋏ where required	𝟨 𝟫 𝟨𝟨 𝟫𝟫

Roman numerals

I	1	XX	20
II	2	XXI	21
III	3	XXX	30
IV	4	XL	40
V	5	L	50
VI	6	XC	90
VII	7	C	100
VIII	8	CC	200
IX	9	D	500
X	10	DCC	700
XI	11	DCCXIX	719
XII	12	CM	900
XIII	13	M	1000
XIV	14	MC	1100
XV	15	MCX	1110
XVI	16	MCMXCI	1991
XVII	17	MM	2000
XVIII	18	MMX	2010
XIX	19		

S

Stockmarket indices

The following is a list of world stockmarket indices.

Americas

Argentina
General

Brazil
Bovespa

Chile
IGPA General

Colombia
CSE Index

Mexico
IPA

Peru
Lima General

Venezuela
IBC

Canada
S&P/TSX Metal & Mining
S&P/TSX Comp
S&P/TSX 60

United States
AMEX composite
DJ Industrials
DJ Composite
DJ Transport
DJ Utilities
S&P 500
NASDAQ Composite
NASDAQ 100
Russell 3000
NYSE Composite
Wilshire 5000

Asia & Australasia

Australia
S&P All Ordinaries
S&P/ASX 200
S&P/ASX 200 Res

China
FTSE/Xinhua A200
FTSE/Xinhua B All-Share
FTSE/Xinhua B35

Hong Kong
Hang Seng
HSCC Red Chip

India
BSE Sens
S&P CNX 500

Indonesia
Jakarta Composite

Japan
2nd Section
Nikkei 225
S&P-Topix 50
Topix

Malaysia
KLSE Composite

New Zealand
NZSX 40

Pakistan
KSE-100

Philippines
Manila Composite

Singapore
SES All-Singapore
Straits Times

South Korea
KOSPI
KOSPI 200

Sri Lanka
CSE All-Share

Taiwan
WeightedPr.

Thailand
Bangkok SET

Europe

Austria
ATX Index

Belgium
BEL20
Brussels Cash

Czech Republic
PX 50

Denmark
KFX

Estonia
Tallinn General

Finland
Hex General

France
CAC 40
SBF 250

Germany
FAZ Aktien
XETRA Dax

Greece
Athens General
FTSE/ASE 20

Hungary
Bux

Ireland
ISEQ Overall

Italy
Banca Com Ital
Mibtel General

Latvia
RIGSE

Lithuania
VILSE

Netherlands
AEX
AEX All Share

Norway
Oslo All-Share

Poland
Wig

Portugal
PSI 20
PSI General

Romania
BET Index

Russia
RTS

Slovakia
Sax

Spain
IBEX 35
Madrid SE

Sweden
OMX Index
Stockholm All Share

Switzerland
SMI Index
SPI General

Turkey
IMKB Nat 100

UK
FTSE 100
FTSE 250
FTSE All-Share
FTSE Small Cap
FTSE techMARK

Middle East & Africa

Egypt
Cairo SE General

Israel
Tel Aviv 100

Jordan
Amman SE

Morocco
MASI

Nigeria
SE All-Share

South Africa
FTSE/JSE All Share
FTSE/JSE Res 20
FTSE/JSE Top 40

Zimbabwe
ZSE Industrial

Cross-border indices
DJ Euro Stoxx 50
DJ Stoxx 50
Euronext 100
FTSE eTX All-Share
FTSE Multinationals
FTSE Global 100
FTSE4Good Global
FTSE E100

FTSE E300
MSCI ACWI Free
MSCI EMU
MSCI Europe
MSCI World
S&P Global 1200
S&P Europe 350
S&P Euro

Source: *Financial Times*

Time of day around the world

Here is a list of countries of the world showing how many hours fast (+) or slow (–) they are relative to Greenwich Mean Time (GMT). The figures show the winter clock time; where summer time is normally observed, the hour is marked with*.

Algeria +1
Angola +1
Argentina –3
Australia
  New South Wales, Canberra,
  Tasmania, Victoria +10*
  Queensland +10
  South Australia +9.5*
  Northern Territory +9.5
  Western Australia +8
Austria +1*
Azerbaijan +4*
Bahamas –5*
Bahrain +3
Bangladesh +6
Belarus +2*
Belgium +1*
Bolivia –4
Brazil
  Fernando de Noronha –2
  Coast & Brasilia –3
  West –4*
Brunei +8
Bulgaria +2*
Canada
  Newfoundland Island –3.5*
  Atlantic –4*
  Eastern –5*
  Central –6*

  Mountain –7*
  Pacific & Yukon –8*
Chile –4*
China, mainland & Hong Kong
  –4*
Colombia –5
Congo
  Katanga, Kivu +2
  Kinshasa +1
Costa Rica –6
Côte d'Ivoire GMT
Croatia +1*
Cyprus +2*
Czech Republic +1*
Denmark +1*
Dominican Republic –4
Ecuador –5
Egypt +2*
Estonia +2*
Ethiopia +3
Finland +2*
France +1*
Germany +1*
Ghana GMT
Greece +2*
Hungary+1*
Iceland GMT
India +5.5
Indonesia

Eastern +9
Central +8
Western +7
Iran +3.5*
Iraq +3*
Ireland GMT
Israel +2*
Italy +1*
Jamaica −5
Japan +9
Kazakhstan
  Eastern +6*
  Central +5*
  Western +4*
Kenya +3
Korea, North & South +9
Kuwait +3
Latvia +2*
Lebanon +2*
Libya +2
Lithuania +2*
Luxembourg +1*
Malaysia +8
Malta +1*
Mexico, Mexico City −6*
Morocco GMT
Netherlands +1*
New Zealand +12*
Nigeria +1*
Norway +1*
Oman +4
Pakistan +5
Panama −5
Papua New Guinea +10
Paraguay −4*
Peru −5
Philippines +8
Poland +1*
Portugal GMT*
Puerto Rico −4

Qatar +3
Romania +2*
Russia
  Moscow +3*
  Omsk +6*
Saudi Arabia +3
Serbia and Montenegro +1*
Sierra Leone GMT
Singapore +8
Slovakia +1*
Slovenia +1*
South Africa +2
Spain +1*
Sweden +1*
Switzerland +1*
Syria +2*
Taiwan +8
Tajikistan +5
Thailand +7
Trinidad & Tobago −4
Tunisia +1
Turkey +2*
Ukraine +2*
United Arab Emirates +4
United Kingdom GMT*
United States
  Eastern −5*
  Central −6*
  Mountain −7*
  Pacific −8*
  Alaska −9*
  Hawaii −10
Uruguay −3
Uzbekistan +5
Venezuela −4
Vietnam +7
Yemen +3
Zambia +2
Zimbabwe +2

index